UP THE
POLITICAL
LADDER

Contemporary American Politics

The **Contemporary American Politics** series is intended to assist students and faculty in the field of American politics by bridging the gap between advanced but oft-times impenetrable research on the one hand, and oversimplified presentations on the other. The volumes in this series represent the most exciting work in political science—cutting-edge research that focuses on major unresolved questions, contradicts conventional wisdom, or initiates new areas of investigation. Ideal as supplemental texts for undergraduate courses, these volumes will examine the institutions, processes, and policy questions that make up the American political landscape.

Books in This Series

DO CAMPAIGNS MATTER?
Thomas M. Holbrook

GENDER DYNAMICS IN CONGRESSIONAL ELECTIONS
Richard Logan Fox

THE CONGRESSIONAL BLACK CAUCUS: Racial Politics in the
U.S. Congress
Robert Singh

POLITICAL TOLERANCE: Balancing Community and Diversity
Robert Weissberg

UP THE POLITICAL LADDER: Career Paths in U.S. Politics
Wayne L. Francis & Lawrence W. Kenny

UP THE POLITICAL LADDER

Career Paths in U.S. Politics

Wayne L. Francis
Lawrence W. Kenny

CONTEMPORARY
AMERICAN
POLITICS

Sage Publications, Inc.
International Educational and Professional Publisher
Thousand Oaks ■ London ■ New Delhi

For information:

Sage Publications, Inc.
2455 Teller Road
Thousand Oaks, California 91320
E-mail: order@sagepub.com

Sage Publications Ltd.
6 Bonhill Street
London EC2A 4PU
United Kingdom

Sage Publications India Pvt. Ltd.
M-32 Market
Greater Kailash I
New Delhi 110 048 India

Printed in the United States of America

Library of Congress Cataloging-in-Publication Data

Francis, Wayne L.
    Up the political ladder: Career paths in U.S. politics / by
Wayne L. Francis & Lawrence W. Kenny.
        p.   cm.—(Sage series on Contemporary American Politics; v. 5)
    Includes bibliographical references (p.) and index.
    ISBN 0-7619-1426-9 (cloth)
    ISBN 0-7619-1427-7 (pbk.)
    1. Politics, Practical—United States.   2. Politics, Practical—
Vocational guidance—United States.   3. Political leadership—United
States.   4. Political leadership—Vocational guidance—United States.
5. Politics, Practical—United States—States.   6. Politics, Practical—
Vocational guidance—United States—States.   7. Career development—
United States.   I. Kenny, Lawrence W.   II. Title.   III. Series.
    JK1726 .F66   2000
    324.7′023′73—dc21   99-6714

This book is printed on acid-free paper.

00   01   02   03   04   05   06   7   6   5   4   3   2   1

Acquisition Editor:	Peter Labella
Editorial Assistant:	Brian Neumann
Production Editor:	Wendy Westgate
Editorial Assistant:	Karen Wiley
Typesetter:	Lynn Miyata
Cover Designer:	Candice Harman

To Barbara and Christine

Contents

Acknowledgments

Several years ago, we began to work individually, together, and with others on topics related to upward political mobility in the United States. We were fortunate enough to publish some of our work in the *American Journal of Political Science, Economic Inquiry, Journal of Politics,* and *Legislative Studies Quarterly.* We thank Richard Niemi and Barbara Sinclair for taking note of this work and asking us to think about a book-sized manuscript that would tie together and expand upon our previous studies. The suggestion could not have been more timely, and it was not long thereafter that we signed on with Sage Publications to produce the manuscript. We should say that although we have utilized our previously published work, much of this effort is new in theme, content, and interpretation.

We are particularly in debt to those with whom we have previously coauthored articles and papers. Becky Morton and Amy Schmidt collaborated with us on two articles examining the role of legislators' voting records in determining (a) whether they seek reelection and their success in getting reelected (Schmidt, Kenny, & Morton, 1996; described in Chapter 5) and (b) whether they seek higher office and are selected as their party's nominee for the general election (Francis, Kenny, Morton, & Schmidt, 1994; summarized in Chapter 6). Bruce Anderson contributed to our study of the initial effects of term limits on legislative turnover (Francis, Kenny, & Anderson, 1998; described in Chapter 4).

We owe special thanks also to Dick Niemi, series editor, whose persistent attention to accurate interpretation and to thematic coherence helped make this a much better book. Our data collections were enhanced with the help of Bruce Anderson and Robert Hogan, who made available information they were collecting on turnover; the Inter-University Consortium on Political and Social Research, from whom we obtained state election data; the College of Business Administration, for providing the resources to collect the congressional data; and Melanie Baker, Ben Blair, Dean Foreman, Tim Hartigan, Cindy Houser, Yikang Li, Samarender Reddy, Scott Roach, Mehmet Sener, and Laixun Zhao, who coded parts of the data set. Although we were in good spirits throughout the writing of this book, never irritable, of course, yet generous with our time, we wish to thank our spouses, Barbara and Christine, who not once suggested that consulting might be more lucrative.

Wayne L. Francis
Department of Political Science
University of Florida

Lawrence W. Kenny
Department of Economics
University of Florida

The Political Ladder and Career Decision Making

What motivates citizens to seek political office rather than some other line of work? In answer to this question, we think it is helpful to view office seekers as those who have relatively strong or better defined opinions on issues and policies and who also see their own political participation as a way to assert and gain acceptance of their views. Such traits set elected officials apart from the rest of the population. National political party convention delegates, for example, compose a great cross-section of political leaders in the United States. Successive samples of their opinions on issues and ideological positions have repeatedly shown far greater party differences on issues than are found between Democratic and Republican identifiers in the mass public (McCloskey, Hoffman, & O'Hara, 1960; Miller & Jennings, 1986). The relative divergence of views of party elites has been further confirmed in a state-by-state analysis by Erikson, Wright, and McIver (1993).

The pursuit of political office in the United States is an open challenge, and any citizen who meets the age requirement and files properly could wage a campaign for public office. To be successful is another matter. Sufficient campaign resources will be needed to win a plurality of votes. Because most

citizens have very limited resources and local races require the least resources, a local office provides the best chance for a successful first political
campaign. Many local offices, including school boards and town and city
councils, have nonpartisan elections in relatively small districts, making it
easier for novices to enter the political arena. Many holders of high office
started their political careers by winning a local, often nonpartisan election.

State and national elections are more difficult to enter and, except for the
Nebraska legislature, are controlled by party nominations. For higher offices,
party organization and politics are more dominant, and winning the Democratic or Republican nomination is nearly a precondition to winning the
general election. To win party caucuses or primaries, candidates must con-
vince the party faithful that they will be effective in representing their
interests. Those who have served in local office are known to many voters
and may have impressed opinion leaders favorably with their performance
in office. As such, they have some advantage in attracting both campaign
contributions and votes in new races for higher office. These advantages lead
many elected officials to pursue a progression up the political career ladder,
increasing their political skills and knowledge and enlarging the set of voters
familiar with them with each rung up the ladder. The decisions to run or not
run for office are crucial career decisions. They are subject to as much careful
consideration and rational forethought as any decisions in one's lifetime.

A Theory of Ambition and the Political Ladder

Men and women with successful political careers often move from one
level of politics to the next. The sequence of offices that many careerists have
held may be referred to as the *political career ladder.* Each move up tends
to be associated with a greater sphere of political power, increased ability to
achieve policy goals, greater financial gain, and possibly increased self-
esteem.[1] Movement up the ladder is characterized by three *ambition principles,* two of which are particularly if not uniquely political.

Three Ambition Principles in Politics

It seems self-evident that as the territorial jurisdiction of the officeholder
increases, the sphere of influence increases also. Thus, for example, a city

council member has a direct effect mainly on the city and its immediate surroundings, whereas a state legislator can affect the practices of the entire state, and a member of Congress can have an effect on the entire country. *Political activists seek to increase their territorial jurisdiction.* That is, they typically seek to rise from local government to state government and ultimately to national government.

A second way to enhance a political career is to directly influence the lives of more citizens. All state legislators, for example, deal with issues affecting the state, but a legislator is expected to represent his or her own district's interests to the legislature when appropriate. The number of voters whose interests are being represented usually increases dramatically with a successful move from the state house to the state senate, or from the state senate to governorship, or from the U.S. House of Representatives to the U.S. Senate (states with one House member excepted), or from the U.S. Senate to the presidency. In essence, *political activists seek to increase the size of their electoral constituency.* Doing so successfully may also offer greater opportunity for activists to convert their preferences into public policy. For example, a member of the Ohio house has a district with only $\frac{1}{99}$ of the state's population. Election to the senate, however, occurs in a district with $\frac{1}{33}$ of the state population. A new state senator in the Ohio 33-member senate chamber has a better chance of influencing committee and chamber decisions than a new member of the 99-member house. The rules of majority voting make it so. The governor of Ohio is in an even better position to convert preferences into policy.

Some moves increase both territorial jurisdiction and the size of the constituency. Moves from the state legislature to Congress increase both.[2] So do moves from mayor to governor or from governor to president. On occasion, a move will increase territorial jurisdiction but reduce the size of the constituency, as when a mayor of a large city runs for a state legislative seat, or when a statewide officeholder runs for a seat in the U.S. House. An increase in territorial jurisdiction may be more valued than a small reduction in constituency size.

Financial gain is a common motivation among officeholders as well as for most other people in our type of economy. *Political activists seek to increase their compensation.* The salary and other compensation offered by a position will influence who will seek the position. It has been established at both national and state levels that salary or income does affect the career decisions of legislators (Brace, 1985; Squire, 1988). A comparison of the median salaries of several offices as of 1997 yields the following:

- Median state legislative salary: $15,000 plus expenses and bonuses
- Median gubernatorial salary: $90,000 plus expenses
- Congressional salary: $133,600 plus expenses
- Presidential salary: $200,000 plus expenses

There is a wide range in salaries among states and among local jurisdictions. Among the states, California legislators have the highest salary ($72,000), and the governor of California also ranks first, earning $131,000, or 46% more than the median governor. New York is a close second. Nevertheless, governors earn noticeably more than state legislators, and elected federal officials are paid more than legislators or governors in any state. House and senate members in a state legislature are generally paid the same salary, and the same is true in Congress. Chamber officers typically are paid a bit more than other members.

Compensation paid to public officials corresponds roughly to the size of the territorial jurisdiction and the size of the electoral constituency. We will find many exceptions, however, especially at the local level. Mayors and city or county council members are sometimes paid more than state legislators, and often the better compensated local officials have a larger constituency. But some state legislatures simply have a long history of very low pay, with part-time rather then full-time obligations. Nevertheless, the overall salary structure in the United States encourages members to seek out offices with a greater electoral constituency and to move to state and federal office.

The Political Ladder

As indicated previously, political actors seek to increase their territorial jurisdiction and the size of their supporting constituency. Taking these dimensions separately first, territorial jurisdiction may be ordered (from low to high) as follows:

- Local jurisdiction (all local elective offices)
- State jurisdiction (all elected offices in state government)
- National jurisdiction (seats in Congress and offices of president and vice president)

Whereas territorial jurisdiction divides neatly into three general categories, size of constituency is more variable. The following classification (again, low to high) suffices here:

- Most local offices (i.e., for smaller cities and counties)
- Seats in state house
- Seats in state senate[3]
- Seats in the U.S. House[4]
- U.S. senatorial and gubernatorial offices
- Offices of the president and vice president

In a rough manner, we can combine the above two dimensions to spell out a number of clear steps on the political ladder, recognizing that there are exceptions and different paths to high office. For the purposes of this book, we focus on the movement of political actors up the political ladder from

- Local office to the state house
- State house to the state senate
- State legislature to the U.S. House
- State legislature or U.S. House to the office of governor
- U.S. House to the U.S. Senate
- U.S. Senate or governor's office to office of the president

Although it is implied that political actors tend to move in the steps indicated, it is clear that some are able to start at a higher level than local office and that others are able to leapfrog intermediate levels of office. The steps are consistent with the goals of political candidates to increase territorial jurisdiction and constituency support, so we assume that the "ladder" reflects the preference ordering of most career politicians.

Movement from local office to the state house increases territorial jurisdiction and usually the size of the constituency. Movement from the state house to the state senate increases size of constituency. Movement from the state legislature to the U.S. House increases territorial jurisdiction in all cases and size of constituency in all but the California senate. Movement from the state legislature to the position of governor increases constituency size. Movement from the U.S. House to governorship does also, but it sacrifices territorial jurisdiction. Movement from the U.S. House to the U.S. Senate increases constituency size, except in states with only one House district. Finally, movement from governor or U.S. senator to president increases constituency size, and governors would also gain in territorial jurisdiction.

A Closer Look at the Elected Offices

Local Office

According to the Bureau of Census, there are approximately 39,000 general-purpose local governments in the United States, including over 3,000 county governments, over 19,000 municipalities, and over 16,000 town or township governments. In addition, there are over 14,000 school districts and over 31,000 other special districts from which officials are elected. The reader may be astonished to learn that there are almost 500,000 *elected* officials serving in local governments, ranging from a school board member in a small rural school district to the mayor of New York City. In addition, there are offices in local Democratic or Republican Party organizations. Local elections are often nonpartisan and may attract many who do not have strong ideological beliefs. For example, parents and teachers with a strong interest in education but no broad political agenda are among those elected to school boards.

State Legislature

The next step up in politics is often the state house. A move to the state house is often attractive because it expands the territorial jurisdiction, providing the potential to directly influence statewide policy. For many, achieving membership in the state house also increases the size of their electoral constituency and results in better compensation.

There are over 5,400 seats in the 49 state lower chambers.[5] The house districts can have rather small populations, but most local elected officials represent even fewer people. For every state house seat, there are nearly 100 local elected officials. Obviously, only a select few move up to the state legislature. Out of the approximately 500,000 local officials, those with stronger views or better defined opinions and those who want to influence policy are likely to enter the more partisan races for higher office. Those who are successful in being elected to state houses are apt to be more ideological and more partisan than those who serve in city and town councils. Nevertheless, as Erikson et al. (1993) pointed out, politicians know enough to temper their stated views to fit within the limits dictated by constituency opinion.

There are over 2,000 state senate seats nationwide. Even though senate members are paid the same and have the same state territorial jurisdiction as house members, they represent, on average, nearly three times as many constituents. As members of a smaller chamber, they also can have, individually, a greater influence on state policy. Thus, we expect that the state "upper" chamber will be preferred to the state house, and there is strong evidence that this is the case. An acid test is the extent to which "sitting" legislators in one chamber decide to run for a seat in the other chamber. An examination of all state legislative elections for 47 states between 1968 and 1986 (Francis, 1993) revealed (a) 1,112 cases of sitting house members challenging directly for a senate seat in the general election and (b) only 18 cases of sitting senators challenging directly for a house seat. Thus, it seems safe to say that most state house members would prefer a state senate seat over a house seat.

U.S. House of Representatives

The U.S. House of Representatives has a greater territorial jurisdiction than does a state legislature, and the typical U.S. House district contains nearly five times as many people as the average state senate district. Congressional salaries also are higher than those found in any state legislature. Consequently, many politicians would prefer a seat in Congress over a seat in the state senate. Consistent with this reasoning, we find that many choose to leave the state legislature to go to Congress. The state legislature has become a natural springboard to the U.S. House. During the 1980s, Canon (1990) found that 49% of the U.S. House of Representatives had prior state legislative experience and that of these 49%, four-fifths had come directly from the state legislature without any intervening experience (p. 53). More recently, the proportion with state legislative experience has exceeded 50% (Berkman, 1994).

Although a seat in the U.S. House has a greater territorial jurisdiction than does a cabinet position in state government, the House seat in all but a handful of states serves a smaller electoral constituency. Apparently, the desire to serve a typically much larger electoral constituency dominates a preference for federal jurisdiction over state jurisdiction. Only 5 of the 435 members of the U.S. House in 1993-1995 had been elected to a state cabinet position. They were three former secretaries of state, one former state attorney general, and one former governor who was precluded by term limits from seeking reelection to that office.

Statewide Office

Politicians can advance to the next rung on the political career ladder by gaining one of several statewide offices: U.S. senator, governor, or perhaps a secondary elected office in state government such as attorney general, secretary of state, state treasurer, or state auditor. These positions offer a greater electoral constituency in all but a few states and give officeholders a greater opportunity to affect policy.

Schlesinger (1966) found that during roughly the first half of this century (1900-1958), only 9% of U.S. senators bypassed Congress's lower chamber and came directly from the state legislature. Three times as many (27%) had moved up from the U.S. House. Canon (1990) reported that 37% of the U.S. senators elected between 1960 and 1987 had previous service in the U.S. House (p. 51). U.S. Senate seats are much sought after by political activists, and members of the House of Representatives may find themselves also competing against present and past governors, the state attorney general, the lieutenant governor, and so on, who reasonably claim to have statewide constituencies.

Recent experience dealing with state issues is more important in becoming governor. Schlesinger found that in the first half of this century 19% of governors entered that office via the state legislature but only 10% of governors did so from being just in the U.S. House. From our own analysis of governors in office from 1988 to 1998, we find that about one-third were legislators, 17% moving up from the state legislature and 15% from the U.S. House.[6] Other statewide elective offices in state government are also important gateways to the governor's mansion. More than one third (37%) of the governors had moved from lieutenant governor, attorney general, secretary of state, treasurer, or auditor, with the majority having served as lieutenant governor. Almost 80% of recent governors had held some elective position (including mayor and U.S. senator).

Presidency

The presidency is, of course, the highest rung on the U.S. political ladder. U.S. senators and governors have the necessary political skills to be well positioned for a presidential race. Because they can energize a statewide electorate, they have some prospect of producing enthusiastic supporters nationwide. Also, the more intense media scrutiny and competitive elections generally found in statewide races help to prepare U.S. senators and governors for a rough-and-tumble presidential race.

As shown in Table 1.1, the major party candidates over the past century have been predominately governors and U.S. senators. Twenty-seven different candidates have been a governor or U.S. senator. Three-quarters of the 16 presidents elected in this century and 68% of the 22 losing major party candidates have held one of these two positions.

Presidential primaries have become more important in selecting each party's nominee. By 1972, a majority of delegates were selected in primaries. The growing importance of presidential primaries should favor candidates with proven vote-getting skills in big races. And perhaps this has made the statewide offices of governor and U.S. senator even more important in the selection of presidential candidates. From 1972 to 1996, all winners of major party nominations for president were former U.S. senators or governors or else vice presidents.

It is clear that the route to the office of the president is through the U.S. Senate or a gubernatorial office. Even vice-presidential candidates have been predominately from the senatorial or gubernatorial ranks. Six of the 10 recent candidates held one of these two positions.[7] Candidates from larger states can deliver more electoral votes and typically have a more diverse electorate that more closely resembles the national electorate. As a result, success campaigning in a large state is more likely to translate into success campaigning in a presidential race. Table 1.1 shows that 11 of the 12 successful presidential candidates who had been a governor or U.S. senator came from

Table 1.1 Winning and Losing Presidential Candidates: Backgrounds as Senators or Governors

Year	Winners				Losers			
	Name	Sen./Gov.	State	Pop. Rank	Name	Sen./Gov.	State	Pop. Rank
1904	T. Roosevelt	Gov.	New York	1	Parker	—	—	—
1908	Taft	—	—	—	Bryan	—	—	—
1912	Wilson	Gov.	New Jersey	11	Taft	—	—	1
					T. Roosevelt[a]	Gov.	New York	1
1916	Wilson	Gov.	New Jersey	11	Hughes	Gov.	New York	1
1920	Harding	Sen.	Ohio	4	Cox	Gov.	Ohio	4
1924	Coolidge	Gov.	Massachusetts	6	Davis	—	—	—
					LaFollette[a]	G&S	Wisconsin	13
1928	Hoover	—	—	—	Smith	Gov.	New York	1
1932	F. Roosevelt	Gov.	New York	1	Hoover	—	—	—
1936	F. Roosevelt	Gov.	New York	1	Landon	Gov.	Kansas	24
1940	F. Roosevelt	Gov.	New York	1	Willkie	—	—	—
1944	F. Roosevelt	Gov.	New York	1	Dewey	Gov.	New York	1
1948	Truman	Sen.	Missouri	10	Dewey	Gov.	New York	1
					Thurmond[a]	Gov.	South Carolina	25
1952	Eisenhower	—	—	—	Stevenson	Gov.	Illinois	4

Year	Winner				Opponent			
1956	Eisenhower	—	—	—	Stevenson	Gov.	Illinois	4
1960	Kennedy	Sen.	Massachusetts	9	Nixon	Sen.	California	2
1964	Johnson	Sen.	Texas	6	Goldwater	Sen.	Arizona	35
1968	Nixon	Sen.	California	2	Humphrey	Sen.	Minnesota	18
					Wallace[a]	Gov.	Alabama	19
1972	Nixon	Sen.	California	2	McGovern	Sen.	South Dakota	45
1976	Carter	Gov.	Georgia	9	Ford	—	—	—
1980	Reagan	Gov.	California	1	Carter	Gov.	Georgia	9
1984	Reagan	Gov.	California	1	Mondale	Sen.	Minnesota	21
1988	Bush	—	—	—	Dukakis	Gov.	Massachusetts	11
1992	Clinton	Gov.	Arkansas	33	Bush	—	—	—
1996	Clinton	Gov.	Arkansas	33	Dole	Sen.	Kansas	32

NOTE: The population rank refers to the census year that governed the allocation of seats to the U.S. House of Representatives, and thus the electoral college.
a. Third-party candidate. Only candidates getting some electoral college votes are included.

11

one of the 11 largest states. In contrast, only 8 of the 15 losing candidates from these offices were from one of the 11 most populous states.

Political Ambition Theory and Decision Making

In the private sector, it is not too difficult to understand job changes and careers. Workers gain knowledge and become more skillful with additional experience working in the labor market. The new skills often result in promotions. Most promotions give workers an increase in earnings that more than compensates for any additional effort required. Consequently, most promotions are accepted, and if advancement within the firm is not adequate, workers can search for other firms that will better reward them for their new skills. A job change may require a move to a different, even distant, city. Then the individual will take the new job if the increase in salary, adjusted for cost-of-living differences, compensates for the cost of moving and the value placed on lost friendships and amenities.

Career decisions involving elective public office, however, are more complicated than most private sector career decisions. There is an inherent uncertainty in running for election to public office. A person aspiring to elective office needs to assess not only the value (or utility) of holding that office but also the probability of winning and the cost of campaigning to obtain the seat.

The Value (or Utility) of the Office

To make career decisions, individuals need to compare the options available to them. In this context, each political aspirant must attach or "assign" a value (or utility) to each office that he or she considers. Different citizens will assign different values, but the only crucial consideration is how the values an individual places on the potential offices compare. The political career ladder was constructed to reflect candidates' typical ordering of elected offices. For example, the U.S. Senate was higher on the political ladder than the state house because most politicians would prefer being a U.S. senator to being a member of a state house. Consistent with this, we assume that *political aspirants will tend to assign higher values to offices higher on the political career ladder than to offices lower on the career ladder.*

The Countervailing Effects of Value Versus Probability of Winning

Because we have argued that the "political ladder" reflects the preference ordering of most elected officials, it follows that if the probabilities of winning the senate and house races are equal and the costs of running the two campaigns are equal, most elected officials will run for the better job—the "higher office." But the costs and probabilities are rarely equal. If we have a political system where the great majority of politicians place higher value on offices higher on the ladder, why are they not challenging upward at every opportunity? It is to a large extent because the lower probability of winning the higher office makes a bid for it less worthwhile.

Thus, we might expect that *as the value attached to higher office rises relative to the value associated with the lower office, a greater number of aspirants will seek higher office.* But conversely, *as the probability of winning a bid for higher office falls relative to the probability of winning reelection, fewer officials will seek higher office.* Consequently, public officials will behave rationally and balance these two considerations in deciding whether to run for higher office or run for reelection. A bid for higher office is worth little if there is almost no prospect of winning the election. For example, a state legislator does not run for president because the probability of winning is near zero. But when a state representative must decide whether to run for the state senate or run for reelection, the choice may not be so easy to make. When there is *uncertainty* about the electoral outcomes, decision-making methods need to be adjusted to take into account the probabilities of experiencing each possible outcome.

Under this condition of uncertainty, actors will tend to seek the position with the greatest expected value. The *expected* value of a decision to run for an office is the sum of the probability-weighted values of the possible outcomes (see the boxed example for a precise formulation). The possible outcomes typically are (a) win the office or (b) return to the private sector. The value of each outcome is weighted by the probability that it will occur, and the results are summed.

A Simple Numerical Example of Choosing Whether to Seek Higher Office

Suppose a state senator associates a value of 20 with holding a seat in the U.S. House, a value of 15 with remaining as a state senator, and a value of 10 with returning to some private sector job. Suppose further that there is an 0.8 probability of winning reelection and an 0.3 chance of winning the higher office. In both cases, an election loss means returning to the private sector.

The expected value of a reelection bid is

$$(P_W \times \text{Value of State Senate Seat}) + (P_L \times \text{Value of Private Sector Job}) =$$
$$(.8 \times 15) + (.2 \times 10) = 14,$$

and the expected value of running for the higher seat is

$$(P_W \times \text{Value of U.S. House Seat}) + (P_L \times \text{Value of Private Sector Job}) =$$
$$(.3 \times 20) + (.7 \times 10) = 13,$$

where P_W and P_L equal the probability of winning the race and probability of losing the race, respectively. The senator would choose reelection in this case because its expected value (14) exceeds the expected value for a bid for higher office (13). Normally, politicians run for reelection because the probability of defeating an incumbent in the higher office is so low.

The Temporizing Effects of Campaign Costs

Candidates for office need to spend money to make more voters aware of their candidacy and to inform voters about their platform and qualifications for office and about those challenging them for the office. Providing the funding necessary for a successful campaign can be difficult. Candidates can spend as much of their own money as they wish, but they are subject to limitations on seeking funds from others in federal elections and in many state elections. These limitations make it more difficult to obtain sufficient contributions from individuals and political action committees (PACs). In expensive campaigns, the candidate must spend more time raising money through phone calls and fund-raising dinners, which can make the office less appealing.

We may thus infer that as the projected cost of running a campaign for higher office rises relative to the campaign costs for seeking reelection, fewer officials will seek higher office. Campaign spending provides a gauge of both the value that donors place on the office and the effort needed for fund-raising. Because the great cost of presidential campaigns is well documented, let us compare typical campaign spending figures (median expenditures) for several lower offices.[8]

	Median Campaign Expenditures	
1994	State Houses in 19 States: Contested Races	$ 30,000
1996	U.S. House:	
	Incumbents	$ 541,000
	Open Seats	$ 596,000
1996	U.S. Senate, All Major Party Candidates	$2,900,000

Hogan and Hamm (1998) reported a wide range in median state house campaign expenditures in the 19 states they examined. In California, expenditures ($438,000) were almost as high as those for the typical U.S. House race. But campaigns were much less expensive in the other states, ranging from $189,000 in Illinois to around $20,000 in Minnesota and Missouri to under $8,000 in Idaho and Wyoming. The U.S. House medians for incumbents and open seats, although higher than those for state house seats, are substantially less than the median for the U.S. Senate. These figures help to substantiate the assertion that a seat in the U.S. Senate is more highly valued than a seat in the U.S. House, which in turn is more valued than a seat in the state house.

It is also clear that moving up the political ladder requires more and more ambitious fund-raising. Some candidates are independently wealthy and will spend part of their estates to obtain high office. Most others, however, will need to rely on contributors, which is more difficult. Thus, many potential candidates do not challenge for higher office, and the rich are much more likely to dominate races for higher office than races for lower office. We (Francis et al., 1994) found that U.S. House members with apparent family wealth were four times more likely to enter a U.S. Senate primary and over eight times more likely to be the party's nominee for the Senate than were U.S. House members with no indication of wealth.

The cost of fund-raising varies not only among levels of office but also among candidates running for the same type of office. Because incumbents get more PAC contributions than their challengers, they face a lower personal cost of campaigning, which encourages a decision to run for reelection in the future. Committee chairs and others in power have an easier time raising PAC contributions and thus are more likely to seek reelection. In sum, *as the personal cost of reelection falls, elected officials are more likely to seek reelection.*

Conclusion

Elected public officials face a periodic decision to make one of three choices: run for higher office, run for reelection, or return to a nonelective position. The framework that we have developed here will help us to better understand the decisions they make. The greater value associated with higher office is the lure that causes politicians to reach for the next rung on the political ladder. Political career decisions, however, involve "strategic" decision making that takes account of electoral success in future years as well as in the current election. Thus, we will see that the low probability of unseating an incumbent leads elected officials to wait for an open seat. And the odds of success are even greater if the official waits for an open election in which there is no serious opposition from other experienced elected officials. As a result, the traditional political career may be characterized as reelection oriented, where candidates build their public support and wait patiently for the ideal chance to move up. The advent of term limits, however, which is discussed in Chapter 4, has forced elected officials to be less selective about their bids for higher office. We will see that in the term limit states, many legislators leave office before they are compelled to do so by the term limits.

Notes

1. The need for self-esteem may lead political activists to seek "higher" office, just as it leads others to seek corporate promotions, to publish, to invent, and so on. But the pursuit of self-esteem provides little insight into how elected offices are ordered on the political ladder.

2. One exception is in California, which now has fewer state senators than representatives in the U.S. House.

3. The California senate has larger districts than U.S. House districts.

4. Because one-seat states have statewide House districts, a movement from the House to the Senate entails no increase in constituency size in these states.

5. Nebraska has only one legislative chamber, which is counted among the state senates.

6. This is based on the biographies found in Mullaney (1994) and on the occupations given in the 1992, 1994, and 1996 candidate lists in *Congressional Quarterly Weekly Reports* ("Candidates," 1992, 1994, 1996).

7. One of the exceptions was R. Sargent Shriver, former director of the Peace Corps, a last-minute replacement for Senator Eagleton of Missouri, who withdrew after being nominated.

8. The national-level data are taken from the Web site reports of the Federal Election Commission. The state data appear in Hogan and Hamm (1998). The median values do hide the more extreme cases. For example, in Virginia in 1996, Mark Warner spent $11.6 million in a losing effort to gain a seat in the U.S. Senate. Senator John Kerry, Democratic incumbent in Massachusetts, spent $10.9 million to retain his seat. That same year, House Speaker Newt Gingrich spent $5.6 million on reelection to his seat in Georgia, and House Minority Leader Richard Gephardt disbursed $3.1 million in his campaign.

Prospects for Success

The Political Landscape in the 50 States

Political careers often begin by working in campus politics, a campaign for a particular ballot proposition, a local school board election, a town or city council race, or a myriad of more exalted campaigns for higher office. At some point, many of the politically aware and politically active may decide to run for office and launch their own political career. To move up the political ladder, most citizens need to climb each step, one at a time, until reaching a level that will satisfy their ambition but not exceed their capability.

Celebrities and wealthy citizens are the most notable exceptions. Canon (1990) identified the celebrities in the title of his book *Actors, Athletes, and Astronauts.* Wealthy citizens sometimes carry a prominent family name or have been influential in the corporate world. Because of their name recognition or reputation for managerial skills, they are often able to vault into a prominent position of power. The state of Ohio, interestingly, has had powerful U.S. senators with little previous political experience who entered politics from both types of nontraditional backgrounds: Howard Metzenbaum, a wealthy business entrepreneur, and John Glenn, the first American astronaut to orbit the earth. Ronald Reagan catapulted from movie actor to governor of California and then to president. Ross Perot, wealthy computer industry entrepreneur, ran a strong third as a presidential candidate. The lower house of Congress has included among its members former athletes Steve Largent and J. C. Watts, entertainer Sonny Bono, and Oliver North, a former lieutenant colonel who gained notoriety as a target of the Iran-Contra investigations.

The visibility of celebrities in politics tends to distort popular images of who makes decisions. Schlesinger (1966) found in his early study of office-holders between 1900 and 1958 that only 8.1% of the governors and 8.2% of the U.S. senators had not held a position in government. Canon (1990) reported that between 1913 and 1984 only 6.1% of U.S. senators were "amateurs" when they entered office and that between 1930 and 1984 only 25.1% of the U.S. House members were.

There is a career ladder that ends in Washington, D.C. Many of those in the nation's capitol have spent a lifetime in politics, working in party organizations and holding successively higher offices in local, state, and national government. They are the career professionals who know how to legislate, negotiate over policy, and maintain majority support in the district. They are the progressively ambitious, as some would say, those who have "made it" to Washington.

Experience Prior to the State Legislature

The 50 states are dissimilar in geography, economy, and political organization, and these differences affect the nature and degree of experience that citizens will have when they enter a race for the state legislature. All who live in New Jersey, for example, are classified as living in a "Standard Metropolitan Area." Only 13 of the 80 legislators in the state's lower chamber reported having no prior elective or appointive office. And 62 house members (78%) held an elective office prior to winning a legislative seat. Many were on town or village councils; others were on school boards, city councils, or county councils. Several had served a term or two as mayor.

For contrast, we can examine a more rural state, such as Kentucky. In Kentucky, most house members do not have significant prior political experience. Only 26 of the 100 members report in their biographical sketch that they have held a prior elective office. Kentucky legislators were active members of their communities, often holding some leadership position connected with the chamber of commerce, Jaycees, church-related activities, charities, farm groups, youth groups, or professional associations. Such community notables are often able to run directly and successfully for the state legislature. No doubt, many of these legislators were active to some degree in party politics, perhaps only making campaign contributions, but they did not hold a government position, elective or otherwise. The Kentucky senate, which has 38 members and larger districts, does exhibit more member experience: About one-third of the members have served in the house, and another one-fourth have held other significant government or party positions.

Why do we have such a difference between New Jersey and Kentucky? In both legislatures, members consider being a representative a part-time job; the New Jersey legislature, however, is more professionalized in the sense that its members receive greater compensation, have more staff, and have longer sessions. New Jersey legislators receive a salary of $35,000, whereas Kentucky legislators receive $100 salary per day plus $75 per day of unvouchered expenses, producing an income of $10,500 if the Kentucky session reaches its limit of 60 days. Thus, the incentives to move out of local office into the state legislature are not as great in Kentucky.[1] Also, New Jersey is a patchwork of 21 counties and over 300 villages, townships, and cities of over 5,000 population, all of which have elected officials. These elected positions in county government and "cities" of some size serve as a kind of testing ground in local government and as stepping-stones to the state legislature. Kentucky, with only about 80 local governments of over 5,000 population in addition to its 120 counties, has fewer positions in the larger local governments to feed into the state legislature.

Table 2.1 illustrates the previous experience of members in several other state houses as well. We may note that New Jersey, Massachusetts, California, and New York are similar in that at least two-thirds of the membership have significant prior political experience or some form of government service. These are highly professionalized state legislatures, ranking in the top 10 in King's (1997) recent update of Peverill Squire's "professionalization index." This is an index that takes the mean of three variables: legislator compensation, length of session, and staff support. Each state is compared to Congress on the same three measures. If a state provides its members 50% of the compensation that members of Congress receive, has sessions only 40% as long as those of Congress, and offers staff support that is only 30% of congressional support, then the state receives a score of 40%, the average of the three percentages.

Table 2.1   Previous Public Service of Legislators Serving in State Houses of
Selected States

State	Estimated District Voting-Age Population	% No Prior Public Service Reported	% Held Local Elective Office	% Held Government Appointment	% Held Political Party Position	Squire Index Rank (1-50)
New Jersey	75,000	16	78	6	—	10
Massachusetts	29,000	28	52	3	17	9
California	290,000	29	38	24	10	1
New York	91,000	32	54	3	11	2
Wisconsin	38,000	40	33	11	14	14
Florida	91,000	48	23	18	11	23
Kentucky	29,000	68	25	1	6	42
Alabama	30,000	86	10	3	1	45

NOTE: Most recent position is counted if more than one is listed. Data are taken from legislative home pages. The absence of political party positions in New Jersey may be due to reporting criteria used by that state, although a very high percentage held an elective office just prior to winning a legislative seat. The Squire ranking is calculated from King (1997) data for 1993-1994.

Moving down the list in Table 2.1 to Wisconsin and Florida, we see that previous significant political experience is lacking in 40% to 50% of the cases, whereas in Kentucky and Alabama, the least professionalized of the state legislatures, a large majority of members appear to be political novices when they first enter. The Alabama pay scale is the lowest of the group, only $10 a day for a limit of 105 days, inducing very few Alabamians to leave other public service positions to join the state legislature.

Another state, Alaska, not shown in this table, ranks in the top 10 in *professionalization* on the Squire index, and indeed, of its 40 members of the state house, only 7 have had no previous political or government experience. Prior experience in Alaska is a bit different from that in other states. Nearly half of the members (18) have served on government boards or commissions of special districts or functions, whereas only 10 have served in a general-purpose local office and another 5 had positions in the Democratic or Republican political party organization. Alaska's vast land mass and complex federal, state, and Native American relationships have spawned a sizable number of special districts and planning/oversight commissions, which provide good training for the state legislature.

In sum, we can see that there is a great deal of variation among the states' assemblies. In some, most newcomers have prior political experience, but in others, a great many new members are novices, entering public office for the first time when they win a seat to the state legislature. Lack of experience is more common in states with low salaries and short sessions or, essentially, in states that are less professionalized. Political inexperience also is more frequent in states with fewer significant local governments that can provide some preparation for the legislature.

Prospects for Advancement

The prospects and opportunities for advancing up the proverbial political ladder vary considerably across the nation. Entering the state legislature is easier in states with house districts serving a small population. Moving up to the state senate is facilitated when there are very few representatives who can compete for a senate seat. Moves to Congress benefit from populous state legislative districts.

Ease of Entry Into State Politics

Travel by auto through New Hampshire or Vermont may lead to a friendly encounter with a state legislator, possibly the attendant who cleans your windshield or accepts your credit card. There are 400 members of the New Hampshire house, each with a district of only about 2,100 residents who are eligible to vote in each district and of even fewer households to contact in a campaign for office. Vermont has only 2,900 eligible voters in a district. North Dakota, Wyoming, Maine, Montana, South Dakota, and Rhode Island also have fewer than 8,000 eligible voters in their house districts. These are states with very easy entry to the state house.

In conspicuous contrast are the California house districts, each of which contains a voting-age population of approximately 290,000. The next largest state house districts are in New York, Texas, and Florida, all of which have about 90,000 per district voting-age population. California is the outlier—the most populous state with a state house of only 80 members and districts of at least 100 times the population of those in New Hampshire or Vermont.

The average citizen will find it much easier to enter politics at the state level when the population of the legislative district is small. For a few hundred dollars, every household in the district in New Hampshire and Vermont can be contacted by mail. In these states, the cost of a campaign to enter the lower chamber of the state legislature is minimal. Moncrief (1998) found that in 1994 the mean expenditure by candidates for the state house was a mere $3,947 in Maine, $5,633 in Montana, and $4,201 in Wyoming. Multiply these figures by 100 in California or by 30 or 40 in Florida, New York, or Texas. Moncrief reported that the mean candidate expenditure for house races in California in 1994 was $322,688, or more than 80 times the cost in an average Maine district (p. 43).

Table 2.2 displays in the first column the states ordered by the voting-age population of house districts. Entry into state politics tends to become progressively more difficult as one moves down the list of states to those with the largest district populations.

There are certainly other factors that affect ease of entry. For example, the geographic areas tend to be quite large in states like Montana, making it more difficult to campaign. Also, the pay incentives are greater in some states, such as Wisconsin, which will attract more competition for the offices.

Nevertheless, the principal hurdle in winning office is favorable name recognition among a sufficient number of voters to win a plurality. As that "sufficient number" requirement increases with district population, fewer and fewer citizens will find it attainable because of the need for ample private resources to mount a respectable campaign. States with the more populous districts do tend to offer higher salaries or pay (correlation = .63), but pay incentives do not put money in the pocket of nonincumbents while they are campaigning.

Moving From the State House to the State Senate

Prospects for moving from the house to the senate in a state will depend in part on how many other house members are eligible for the senate seat. How many other "quality" opponents can throw their hats in the ring? A "quality" opponent is generally considered to be someone who has substantial name recognition and the resources to mount a serious campaign (see Bond, Covington, & Fleisher, 1985; Copeland, 1989; Jacobson & Kernell,

Table 2.2   Classification of States According to Career Prospects at Different Levels

States	Ease of Entry: Mean State House District Population[a]	State House Seats per Senate District	State House Move to Senate Rating	State Senate Seats per U.S. House District	State Senate Move to U.S. House Rating	No. of U.S. House Districts
New Hampshire	2,108	16.7	D	12.0	VD	2
Vermont	2,860	5.0	D	30.0	VD	1
North Dakota	4,765	2.0	E	49.0	VD	1
Wyoming	5,717	2.0	E	30.0	VD	1
Maine	6,166	4.3	D	17.5	VD	2
Montana	6,230	2.0	E	50.0	VD	1
South Dakota	7,457	2.0	E	35.0	VD	1
Rhode Island	7,640	2.0	E	25.0	VD	2
Alaska	10,725	2.0	E	20.0	VD	1
Idaho	11,471	2.0	E	17.5	VD	2
Delaware	13,024	2.0	E	21.0	VD	1
West Virginia	13,890	2.9	E	11.3	VD	3
Kansas	15,112	3.1	E	10.0	D	4
Mississippi	15,614	2.3	E	10.4	D	5
Connecticut	16,464	4.2	D	6.0	M	6
Utah	16,613	2.6	E	9.7	D	3
New Mexico	16,671	1.7	E	14.0	VD	3
Hawaii	17,647	2.0	E	12.5	VD	2
Arkansas	18,170	2.9	E	8.8	D	4
Iowa	21,120	2.0	E	10.0	D	5
South Carolina	22,097	2.7	E	7.7	D	6
Oklahoma	23,703	2.1	E	8.0	D	6
Missouri	23,939	4.8	D	3.8	M	9
Nebraska[a]	24,362	—	—	16.3	VD	3
Minnesota	25,090	2.0	E	8.4	D	8

(Continued)

Table 2.2   Continued

States	Ease of Entry: Mean State House District Population[a]	State House Seats per Senate District	State House Move to Senate Rating	State Senate Seats per U.S. House District	State Senate Move to U.S. House Rating	No. of U.S. House Districts
Nevada	25,905	2.0	E	10.5	D	2
Maryland	26,596	3.0	E	5.9	M	8
Massachusetts	28,525	4.0	D	4.0	M	10
Kentucky	28,570	2.6	E	6.3	M	6
Georgia	28,661	3.2	E	5.1	M	11
Louisiana	29,524	2.7	E	5.6	M	7
Alabama	29,886	3.0	E	5.0	M	7
Wisconsin	38,151	3.0	E	3.7	M	9
Oregon	38,516	2.0	E	6.0	M	5
Tennessee	39,525	3.0	E	3.7	M	9
Washington	40,816	2.0	E	5.4	M	9
Colorado	42,391	1.9	E	5.8	M	6
Indiana	42,980	2.0	E	5.0	M	10
North Carolina	44,700	2.4	E	4.2	M	12
Pennsylvania	45,379	4.1	D	2.4	E	21
Arizona	48,717	2.0	E	5.0	M	6
Virginia	49,670	2.5	E	3.6	M	11
Michigan	63,482	2.9	E	2.4	E	16
Illinois	73,831	2.0	E	3.0	E	20
New Jersey	74,675	2.0	E	3.1	E	13
Ohio	83,970	3.0	E	1.7	E	19
Florida	90,467	3.0	E	1.7	E	23
Texas	90,813	4.8	D	1.0	E	30
New York	90,973	2.5	E	2.0	E	31
California	290,313	2.0	E	0.8	E	52

a. Voting-age populations are utilized. Nebraska is unicameral: Estimates apply to the single chamber. Key: E, easy; M, moderately difficult; D, difficult; VD, very difficult.

1981; Krasno & Green, 1988; Squire, 1989; Stewart, 1989). Other members of the legislature certainly qualify as quality opponents. They have an electoral base and usually better access to campaign funding than nonlegislators.

Thus, although in New Hampshire it is fairly easy to become a member of the state house, it would seem most difficult to move up to the senate because there are about 17 house members for each senate district. A house member there has many quality opponents to worry about—that is, other house members who may challenge in the primary as well. Furthermore, the senate district is much larger than the representative's house district and contains many voters unfamiliar with the legislator's record.

The second column in Table 2.2 contains the ratio of house seats to senate seats. Several of the New England states have very small senates and large houses, although the differences are not as extreme as in New Hampshire. In Vermont, Maine, Connecticut, and Massachusetts, there are 4 to 5 house members for every state senator. But Texas, Missouri, and Pennsylvania also have similar attributes. The classification in the third column suggests that in these eight states, with 4 to 17 representatives per senator, it is difficult to advance to the state senate.

In the remaining states, it is easier to move up to the senate. Many states have close to a 3:1 house-to-senate ratio. Seventeen states have exactly two house members for each senator, meaning that the house districts are half the population of the senate districts, and four other states are very close to this 2:1 ratio. Challenging for a senate seat is easiest in New Mexico, where there are only 1.7 house districts for each senate district. In these states, a candidate who wishes to run for the state senate is in a very good position. Normally, there will be only one other state house member who can challenge for the same senate seat. With only one potential house competitor, a legislator often can move up if patient. That is, if there are no term limits, the two members will simply wait until the senate seat is open, assess each other's voting strength, and either let the stronger candidate run or, more rarely, compete with each other for the seat.

Moving From the State Legislature to the U.S. House

As government has become more complex, the state legislature has become a natural stepping-stone to the U.S. House of Representatives. Ease of movement to Congress, however, varies dramatically across the states. The ratio of state senate to U.S. House districts is given in Column 4 of Table 2.2. In California, there is a most unusual situation, where there are fewer state senate districts than House districts. Less well known, perhaps, is the Texas case, where state senate districts and U.S. House districts serve roughly the same number of people. In Ohio, Florida, and New York, there are fewer than two state senate districts for each House district. In all these states, it is relatively easy to move from the state legislature to Congress, for each state senator will be running from a district that encompasses much of the House district. It is still fairly easy to move to the U.S. House in Pennsylvania, Illinois, and New Jersey, where there are between two and three senators for each U.S. House seat. These states, together with the five discussed above, are classified in Column 5 as having an easy move from the state senate to Congress.

At the other end of the continuum, we have states in which everyone in the state senate is in the same House district: Alaska, Delaware, Montana, North Dakota, South Dakota, Vermont, and Wyoming. For these states, the seat in the House of Representatives is a statewide office, with a district and electorate as large as that of the governor and U.S. senators. A congressional campaign here clearly involves much greater costs than a campaign for the state senate. More important, because there are so many eligible opponents (from the entire state senate), it will be very difficult to move to a House seat. These states, with 21 to 50 senators potentially vying for a House seat, and other states having over 11 senate seats for each House seat are classified as having very difficult mobility from the state senate to Congress. In these House races, something is generally needed to distinguish one candidate from the pack; clearly, members in the legislative leadership will have an advantage over other legislators (assuming they receive favorable press).

Generally, in highly populated states, the prospects are bright for members who wish to move from the state senate to the House of Representatives. If they have substantial majority support in their senate districts, the chances are good that they can parlay that support into a victory in a House race. The smaller the state's population, the more difficult it is to reach national office. On the other hand, it is typically easier to enter the state legislature in smaller states. The relationship between the difficulty of entering the state legislature and of moving to Congress is depicted in Table 2.3. The clustering of states along the off-diagonal confirms the inverse relationship between ease of entry into the state legislature and ease of movement to Congress. We need to see this in perspective, of course. It is never really easy to win a House seat, especially against an incumbent, but when a seat does open up, the state senators in states with large districts have a golden opportunity to challenge successfully.

Table 2.3 further delineates the difficulty of advancing from the state house to the U.S. House. In some states, noted with a superscript "a" and scattered throughout the table, it is difficult to move up to the state senate before challenging for Congress.

Moving From the U.S. House to Statewide Office

A member of a 435-seat chamber is not necessarily as happy as a mouse in a cheese factory. It takes years to gain enough seniority to achieve a position of power. Statewide offices can look rather attractive in comparison. The office of the governor, the state office of attorney general, and the U.S. Senate may look especially attractive.

Each cell in the last column in Table 2.2 contains the number of U.S. House districts in the state and represents the number of potential competitors in the House for a statewide position. We can see that seven states, those with the smallest populations, have only one seat in the U.S. House, so that the U.S. representatives share the same electorate with the U.S. senators—or the governor, for that matter. Six additional states have only two House seats, each of which represents 50% of the population of the state. In these states, a move from House to Senate or other statewide office appears relatively easy, for no more than two House members can vie for a statewide position.

By contrast, in the most populous states, there are many House members who can compete against each other. California has 52 House members, New York has 31, and Texas has 30. In these large states, the scenario is not too rosy for the typical progressively ambitious House member. Normally, the officeholder starts with a substantial support base from the home district, but that support does not provide much help in a state with over 20 congressional districts. Because a House member also may have little name recognition much beyond the district, outsiders pose a threat. House members may possibly transcend these problems by gaining publicity in office—say, by becoming part of the House leadership, or by speaking out on popular issues—but it can be difficult to compete against the names of Bush and

Table 2.3 Relationship Between Difficulty of Entry Into State Legislature and Difficulty of Advancement to Congress

Difficulty of Entry Into State Legislature	Easy Move to Congress	Moderately Difficult Move to Congress	Difficult Move to Congress	Very Difficult Move to Congress
Easy entry into state legislature: states with small house district populations; pop. < 14,000				North Dakota Wyoming Montana South Dakota Rhode Island Alaska Idaho Delaware West Virginia New Hampshire[a] Vermont[a] Maine[a]
States with moderate-size house district populations; 15,000 < pop. < 43,000		Maryland Kentucky Georgia Louisiana Alabama Wisconsin Oregon Tennessee Washington Colorado Indiana Connecticut[a] Missouri[a] Massachusetts[a]	Kansas Mississippi Utah Arkansas Iowa South Carolina Oklahoma Minnesota Nevada	New Mexico Hawaii Nebraska
Difficult entry into state legislature: states with large house district populations; 44,000 < pop.	Michigan Illinois New Jersey Ohio Florida New York California Pennsylvania[a] Texas[a]	North Carolina Arizona Virginia		

a. Difficult to move from state house to state senate because of large number of "quality" candidates (i.e., other house members in senate district).

Kennedy or the wealth and celebrity status of other opponents. Celebrities and wealthy candidates who have not held prior office often have a better shot at winning.

Governors and U.S. senators have equivalent electorates, and they can and do move back and forth. As fate would have it, Florida between 1990 and 1998 had former Governor Bob Graham serving as a U.S. senator and former U.S. Senator Lawton Chiles serving as the governor. Also, Pete Wilson left the Senate to become governor of California, and Lowell Weicker successfully campaigned for governor after he was defeated in his bid for a fourth term in the Senate. According to Canon (1990), 14% of senators elected between 1960 and 1987 had been governors. Our analysis of recently elected governors, however, shows that only 3% had been U.S. senators.

Thus, the movement is predominantly from governor to U.S. senator. The governors in a majority of states have term limits, and when those limits force them out, they may return to the private sector, seek an appointment in Washington, run for the U.S. Senate, or campaign for president. If they wish to stay in public office, the Senate is an obvious choice. Bob Graham of Florida and John Ashcroft and Kit Bond of Missouri, for example, became U.S. senators after term limits precluded their remaining as governors.

Governors' salaries also play some role. Their salaries are higher in large states than in small states, but all U.S. senators are paid the same salary. As a result, governors in smaller states have a greater incentive to run for the Senate. Adams and Kenny (1986) reported that the governors' mobility rate to the Senate was 70% higher in small states than in large states.

Leapfrog Challenges

There are a variety of ways in which politicians leapfrog up the traditional ladder. It is common, especially in the more rural states, for prominent citizens to enter directly into the state senate with no previous office experience. Their name recognition and leadership in the community make them formidable candidates. Similarly, others who have done well in business (e.g., John Sununu in New Hampshire, Edward Schafer in North Dakota, Kirk Fordice in Mississippi, and Gaston Caperton in West Virginia) often have been able to argue successfully that they have acquired the skills needed to be governor. Ten percent of governors in office from 1988 to 1998 came from a business background. This argument appears to be more persuasive in states where the governor's job is less demanding. Most of those elected to this position from business came from one of the less populated states (i.e., smaller than Kentucky).

Others more conventionally bypass the state legislature by showing their ability to run a major city or county (e.g., Donald Schaeffer from Baltimore, Maryland; George Voinovich from Cleveland, Ohio; and Bob Martinez from Tampa, Florida). Seven percent of recently elected governors have been a mayor or county executive, and most of these come from one of the three largest cities or counties in the state. They bring a sizable electoral support base and have been able to persuade other voters in the state that they are capable of governing even a large state.

State house members are much less likely than state senators to run for Congress, but some house members bypass the senate in their bid for the U.S. House. The most obvious case is when the state house member has risen to speaker or majority leader. To then become only a rank-and-file state senator would seem to be a move down rather than up. The loss of power is obvious. So a try for Congress or a statewide office seems more appropriate for a house leader. A speaker or majority leader in the house has the advantage of greater media attention and proven leadership skills and thus may have a fair shot at winning a congressional race, especially in states where the house districts constitute a substantial proportion of the congressional district. Because some states redistrict without adhering to the borders of higher or lower offices, there are occasions when a state house district is wholly within the congressional district and will be about as well situated as the senate districts that merely overlap into the congressional district. Because California has by far the largest state house districts, it is the easiest state for representatives to draw on their state house constituency in a race for the U.S. House. In that state, a state house district has about 65% of the population of a U.S. House district. For example, in the 1986, 1994, and 1996 U.S. House races, all the California candidates from the state legislature came from the state assembly (house).

Leapfrogging has been common among presidents, perhaps some of our most ambitious and talented politicians. A few were successful in some endeavor before they ran for public office, and many came from families with at least moderate wealth. As a consequence, they had the name recognition and/or financial resources to seek a position above the beginning level. Some simply took unusual risks in their climb to the top of the political ladder.

Listed below are the first elective offices of 17 presidents elected beginning in 1904:

Local Government	William Taft
	Calvin Coolidge
	Harry Truman
State Legislature	Theodore Roosevelt (house)
	Warren Harding (senate)
	Franklin D. Roosevelt (senate)
	Jimmy Carter (senate)
U.S. House	John Kennedy
	Lyndon Johnson
	Richard Nixon
	Gerald Ford
	George Bush
Statewide	Woodrow Wilson (governor)
	Ronald Reagan (governor)
	Bill Clinton (attorney general)
President	Herbert Hoover
	Dwight Eisenhower

Three recent presidents began their careers unremarkably at the local level. Harry Truman provides the only real example of leapfrogging in this group. He, like the mayors and county executives discussed earlier, was able to move from a similar position (presiding judge) in Missouri's second largest county to the U.S. Senate.

Four presidents began in the state legislature. Teddy Roosevelt's start in the New York state house was not that uncommon. On the other hand, Warren Harding, Franklin Roosevelt, and Jimmy Carter showed more audacity by launching their careers in the state senate.

Remarkably, 10 of the 17 presidents entered politics at even higher offices. Recall that only a quarter of those elected to the U.S. House have been political amateurs. Presidents Johnson, Kennedy, Nixon, Ford, and Bush were first elected to office to this chamber. Bush was even bolder than it might appear, running unsuccessfully for the U.S. Senate before settling on a safe Republican seat in the U.S. House. What facilitated their lofty entry? Lyndon Johnson was able to draw on a favorable reputation that he established as director of the National Youth Administration in Texas. John Kennedy and George Bush both came from wealthy families, and Kennedy also was a best-selling author and war hero. Gerald Ford was a football star at the University of Michigan. In this group, only Richard Nixon had no obvious advantage to offset his political inexperience.

Woodrow Wilson, Ronald Reagan, and Bill Clinton were to start their careers in statewide office. Bill Clinton took many risks in his career. Like Nixon, he had no wealth or fame to offset the disadvantage of beginning his career in a high office. He first lost a race for the U.S. House but later campaigned successfully to become the Arkansas attorney general and 2 years later was elected governor. Only 8% of governors had no experience in government. Woodrow Wilson perhaps was able to take advantage of his fame as a scholar and as president of Princeton University when he ran successfully for governor of New Jersey. Similarly, Ronald Reagan's career in film and television was an asset in his successful bid to be governor of California.

Of all the 20th-century presidents, only Republicans Hoover and Eisenhower did not hold prior elective office. Hoover held administrative positions, rising to Secretary of Commerce, which he held for 8 years before running for president. Eisenhower rose through the military ranks to become supreme Allied commander in Europe and later commanded the NATO forces in Korea before resigning to enter the 1952 presidential race with a promise to end the conflict.

Many politicians move up step by step, but presidents have tended to find a quicker way to the top. The evidence on presidential candidate's career patterns suggest that most are political risk takers. Paul Abramson, John Aldrich, and David Rohde (1987) found that U.S. Senate candidates for president were more likely than other U.S. senators to have a history of risk taking in elections. They were more likely to have gained office by defeating an incumbent or by winning in a state favorable to the other party. When we examine presidents, we see how few really began at the bottom in politics and took the safe way up. Major leaps to high office are more typical than atypical.

Conclusion

In sum, movement from local office to the state legislature appears more common in the more populous states and in states with more professionalized legislatures, where the the perks are ample, the salaries are high, and the time commitment is more demanding. In another sense, those who enter the state legislature from local office are more likely than novices to see public service as a career and may well demand that the legislature become more professionalized. Professionalization may thus arise out of the process of interaction between the development of expectations in local office and the enactment of state legislative benefits that further attract local officeholders.

Finally, in the most populated states, it is much more difficult to make it to the state legislature, relatively easy to move from the state senate to Congress, and very difficult to make it from the U.S. House to the Senate or governorship. Yet leapfrogging up the political ladder is not uncommon, especially for those who have wealth, fame, or managerial skills that can be transferred to political office; leapfrogging is much more common among presidents than among typical politicians.

Note

1. The voting-age population served by the average New Jersey district is about 75,000, two and a half times the size of a Kentucky house district (29,000), and the sessions tend to be longer, so increased compensation would seem justified.

3

Selectivity in Career Decisions
to Move Up

O ne of the more interesting puzzles in political science is that of explaining why candidates win or lose elections. Attempts to solve this complex puzzle have taken several forms. One approach is to examine how effectively candidates raise and spend funds to increase their visibility and to amplify issues that will gain them votes. A second approach is to measure the extent to which voting outcomes are affected by external conditions, such as the health of the economy. A third approach is to evaluate the effects of personal attributes of the candidates on who wins. These approaches complement each other and may be combined in the same analysis. A fourth approach, one that is emphasized in this chapter, is to examine the degree of *selectivity* that various candidates exercise in their decision to seek office. Potential candidates take into account many of the factors elicited in the first three approaches in deciding whether to run for office. By selecting the appropriate races, they raise the odds of their electoral success.

The first way to attack the puzzle of why candidates win or lose is to evaluate what candidates actually do to win votes, including their competitive and reactive behavior in the campaign. Data on campaign spending, media coverage, and issue strategy are central to this approach. Scientific evidence as well as experience has shown that the candidate who spends more usually wins (e.g., see Cassie & Breaux, 1998, for evidence on "contested" state legislative elections, and Green, 1996, on "open" congressional seats). Democratic and Republican strategists alike are often consumed by these concerns. How much money must be raised to win an election? How does the team go about raising such funds? Is the incumbent unbeatable no matter how much money is spent? Can free and favorable media attention be stimulated? On what issues is the opponent weak? How much will negative advertising cost, and will it work? What will the opponent do in retaliation? How does the team buy enough media time in advance to ward off potential attacks from the opponent? Clearly, many potential candidates will consider these questions before deciding whether to run for office. They want to know whether they can raise enough dollars to win and whether issue tactics will work in their favor.

A second way of understanding why candidates win is to evaluate the influence of external conditions, those that are often beyond the full control of the candidates, such as the state of the economy, the partisan nature of the districts, the popularity of candidates higher on the ticket, or even inter-national conditions that help or hinder those in office. For example, the candidate of the "out party" can win more votes if the economy is in bad shape or if the composition of the district changes due to migration or redistricting. It may also make a difference if it is a presidential election year versus an off-year or if a popular governor is running. Legislative candidates sometimes can take advantage of a "coattail" effect by being in the same party as a popular presidential or gubernatorial candidate, or conversely suffer the consequences of an unpopular candidate (see Campbell, 1993). The winning presidential party tends to pick up U.S. House seats, but 2 years later the incumbent president's party often loses House seats in off-year elections. Here again, potential candidates will make an assessment of these influences prior to deciding whether to run for office.

Candidates' characteristics compose a third set of influences on who wins the election. We will see that incumbents have a considerable advantage in winning elections. The relevant political experience of the candidates is also important. "Quality" candidates are often thought to be those with political experience, visibility, and appropriate occupational training—for example, in law (e.g., see Jacobson & Kernell, 1981; Squire, 1989). Their visibility in the community, personality, race, gender, and so on also may affect their ability to attract funds and garner votes. Potential candidates may consider their own qualifications and attributes relative to those of likely opponents as they decide whether to run for office.

Rational Selectivity

There is another question of winning and losing, however, that comes prior to waging the actual campaign and is more important for understanding who moves up the political ladder: the question "Why are candidates in Group A more successful than candidates in Group B?" The answer may well be that the candidates in Group A are more selective in choosing when they will run for office. That is, citizens make rational strategic decisions to run or not run for office. Some may win more than others, not necessarily because they are better campaigners but rather because they are more selective in choosing when to run. They enter only those races where their odds of success are quite high.

The selectivity that legislators show in seeking higher office may be clarified by examining two key determinants of this decision: (a) the likelihood of winning each office (i.e., relative probabilities) and (b) the negative consequences of losing in an election for office.

Likelihood of Winning

Potential candidates assess the likelihood of winning before running for office, and they compare one office against another in determining what action to take. One of the most crucial factors for potential candidates is whether they will be challenging for an open seat: that is, a seat without an incumbent seeking reelection. Incumbents have been highly successful in winning reelection. In the initial election, the legislator was able to gain the name recognition and voter support on issues to have won a majority. With additional experience and exposure, greater access to campaign funding, and the perks of the office that allow greater contact with voters, most officeholders become even more difficult to defeat. These factors make an incumbent a formidable opponent. Thus, it seems reasonable to posit that *in most situations, legislators will estimate that they have a greater probability of winning a higher office if the seat is open.*

By the same token, the legislator who entertains running for higher office is the incumbent of his or her own seat and in that capacity takes on the role of the "formidable opponent." *Thus, in most situations, legislators will estimate that the probability of winning election to a higher office, open or not, is less than the probability of reelection.*

Legislators are not novices, and they will recognize that incumbents have the best chance of winning, that challengers for an open seat have the second best chance of winning, and that challengers to an incumbent have the least chance of winning. Only most unusual circumstances would persuade legislators that they have a higher probability of winning higher office than that of winning reelection as an incumbent.

The evidence supports this reasoning. In Fowler's (1979) interview study of congressional candidates, for example, only 4 of 27 challengers to incumbents thought their chances were "good" or "excellent," whereas for open seats 9 of 16 candidates were optimistic (p. 407). At the state level, we find that incumbents frequently run unopposed, suggesting that potential opponents readily perceive the low odds of winning against an incumbent. In a recent study of a variety of states over four elections, Jewell and Breaux (1988) showed that for each chamber in each of 13 states, the proportion of uncontested seats is substantially higher when incumbents are running.

Open seats are created for a variety of reasons, such as the death or ill health of the incumbent, redistricting, a scandal, and voluntary exiting, the latter often because the incumbent decides to run for a higher office. Exceptions granted, there is little evidence to suggest that seats become open very often because of specific threats from below—that is, threats by specific individuals to challenge for the seat. Thus, we may view open and occupied seats as typically "nonreactive" components of the electoral setting.

When a seat is open, there is yet another factor affecting selectivity—the quality of the likely opponents. In considering a challenge for higher office, a legislator will worry about the quality of the competition in the primary and in the general election. When it appears that there will be an open seat available, the skirmishing among "quality" candidates can be intense. In such a circumstance, as explained in the previous chapter, the natural foes of a legislator are often other legislators within the district of the same higher office. Depending on the level of office, however, other quality opponents, such as a mayor or governor, can also enter the picture.

The odds of winning in an open race depend, of course, on how qualified the candidate's opponents may be. A legislator typically is much more likely to beat a political unknown than to defeat a "quality" opponent because the "quality" opponent has name recognition, likely sources of funding, political experience that may be valued by the electorate, and prior success in winning elections. Open elections against "quality" opponents such as other legislators from the same chamber are less likely to be successful than against other candidates.

Legislators are expected to exercise selectivity in seeking higher office in accordance with the previously noted principles. Generally, they will continue to seek reelection as incumbents until there is an open seat for higher office. Even an open seat offers some risk if they must run against another experienced legislator or some other "quality" opponent. Selectivity in seeking higher office often means waiting until an open race with no serious opposition from other "quality" candidates.

Negative Consequences

In the states, house members are seldom able to retain their seats while running for the senate. Thus, if they lose in a bid for higher office, they may revert to a nonelected job, such as a law practice. On the other hand, in most states it is possible to retain the senate seat if the senator attempted unsuccessfully to move up to Congress at midterm. These differences in negative consequences (noted by Fowler, 1979) can be a determining factor in the career decisions of legislators.

The only broad-based look at these consequences appeared in a brief piece by Hain, Roeder, and Avalos (1981) that examined decisions of state senators in 12 states in which it was possible to retain the senate seat if the senator attempted unsuccessfully to move up to Congress at midterm. Senators were more than twice as likely to run for higher office at midterm because they did not need to risk their seats.

Because risking a house seat to run for the senate involves more undesirable risks (compared to running at midterm), house members should choose to do so only if the odds of winning are higher. Hain et al. (1981) found that when senators did risk their seats, they were indeed more successful, suggesting greater selectivity in choosing which house race to enter. State house members, in contrast, almost always risk their seats when they challenge up, thus requiring a different empirical test of their selectivity.

In the following sections, three types of career decisions are examined: (a) decisions to move from the state house to the state senate; (b) decisions to move from the state legislature to Congress; and (c) decisions to move from the U.S. House to the U.S. Senate. At each level, we can evaluate evidence of legislator selectivity in making career decisions. Previous studies have suggested that quality candidates, mainly those who hold office, are more likely to challenge upward for open seats and overall to fare better than other candidates (see Jacobson & Kernell, 1981, for U.S. House elections and Squire, 1989, for U.S. Senate elections). Here we use a study (Francis, 1993) that covers movement from state houses to state senates, based on data on general elections from 1968 to 1986, a period prior to when legislative term limits were enacted in many states. For movement to Congress, data on primaries are available from an earlier study by Robeck (1982), and we add more recent primary and general election data for select years. U.S. House to U.S. Senate movement in primaries and general elections is evaluated over a 30-year period.

State House to State Senate Decisions

In this section, we suggest that selectivity is an important if not dominant factor in the decisions of state house members to run for the state senate. Although our period of study here is prior to when legislative term limits became popular, even now 32 states do not have state legislative term limits and should continue to exhibit the career behavior found in the earlier period. The most distinguishing feature of this early house-to-senate movement in the states is the extraordinary success of house members. When they do run, they win in over four-fifths of their general election campaigns for open seats. Perhaps more impressive, they win in over two-thirds of their general election races against senate incumbents. Their success is explained principally by "rational selectivity."

For 47 states in the 1970-through-1986 period, approximately 10,000 senate seats were up for election, and about one-fourth or 25% of such elections were for open seats.[1] Francis (1993) found that sitting house members ran in general elections for an open senate seat about 30% of the time such opportunities arose, and that in only 3% of the races a house member ran against an incumbent.[2] From the state election data, it is possible to distinguish among three categories of nonincumbent candidates:

1. Sitting house members
2. Former house members (those out of office at least one term)
3. Other candidates[3]

Table 3.1   Bids for Open Seats or to Unseat Incumbents: First-Time General
Election Challenges for State Senate Seats, 1970 to 1986

Type of Seat	% House Members	% Former House Members	% Other Challengers
Open seat	78	56	41
Incumbent opponent	22	44	59
N	1,073	396	10,137

NOTE: Data were obtained through the Inter-University Consortium for Political and Social Research collection on state elections. Accurate data were not available for Vermont and Minnesota, and Nebraska is unicameral. Cases not counted here include also senate incumbents running against each other due to redistricting. Also, there is a small but undetermined number of cases in which spelling inconsistencies in the records cannot be picked up by a software routine that matches alphabetic names.

Truly remarkable differences are found in the choices made by these types of candidates.

As may be observed in Table 3.1, sitting house members ran for an open senate seat on 78% of their challenges. Former house members ran for an open seat on 56% of their challenges for senate seats, whereas "others" challenged for an open senate seat only 41% of the time. Essentially, house members appear to be more selective; because more of the races they enter are for open seats, they pass up more races against incumbents. House members, we may surmise, demand a higher probability of winning before they choose to run for a senate seat.

From the data at hand, we do not know who entered the state senate primaries without making it to the general election, but normally the easiest primaries to win are those in the opposite party of the incumbent. Yet only about one-fifth of the house candidates who won nomination had won in these "easy" primaries, implying that representatives often wait until an open senate race.

Further startling evidence bearing on legislative career decisions can be obtained by examining the success rates of candidates running under varying conditions. In Table 3.2, challengers for state senate seats are divided into the same three groups. House members won open senate seats 87.2% of the time, ex-house members won 65.5% of the time, and other challengers were successful only 41.8% of the time. Even against incumbents, house members succeeded, incredibly, in two-thirds (67.4%) of the cases, whereas former

Table 3.2   Success of First-Time General Election Bids for State Senate Seats

Type of Seat	% (No.) House Members	% (No.) Former House Members	% (No.) Other Challengers
Open seat	87.2 (837)	65.5 (220)	41.8 (4,144)
Incumbent opponent	67.4 (236)	16.5 (176)	9.8 (5,993)
All	82.8	43.7	22.9

NOTE: See Table 3.1 for data qualifications. Percentages are rates of success.

house members and other challengers were victorious in only 16.5% and 9.8%, respectively, of the races against incumbents. These extraordinary differences testify not only to the greater success of house members who challenge for senate seats but also to their selectivity.

The data presented in Tables 3.1 and 3.2 clearly depict two ways in which house members are selective: in their more frequent challenges for open seats rather than against incumbents and in their more frequent selection of winning situations. We will show next that the data also indicate that house members seldom face each other in open-seat contests.

Why are these state house members so much more selective than other senate candidates? First, house members have a better alternative than other challengers in that they most likely can win reelection and retain their house seat, and thus at least stay in public office. In this sense, they can afford to be choosy. Second, they have more to lose! To run for the senate, they need to give up their house seats. *Relative to possible gains, the possible losses in value (or utility) to house challengers for senate seats typically are greater than they are for other challengers.*

A house seat is the next best thing to a senate seat. If they lose a senate seat challenge, they not only lose that seat but also forfeit the house seat. As noted, state senators preferred to challenge for Congress at their senate midterm, when the negative consequences were less. State house members have no such choice. Thus, they prefer to wait for an open seat before challenging for the state senate. And just as state senators who risked their seats were more successful than those who ran for Congress at midterm, house members in the states were more successful in running for a state senate seat than those challengers who did not need to risk a seat.

Table 3.3   Percentage of Vote Received by Challengers for State Senate Seats, 1970 to 1986

% Vote	% Nonmember Against Incumbent Senator[a]	% Nonmember Running for Open Senate Seat	% House Member Against Incumbent Senator	% House Member Running for Open Senate Seat
5-9.99	3.8	2.6	.6	—
10-19.99	6.8	3.7	—	.4
20-29.99	16.8	8.3	.6	.1
30-39.99	34.0	18.5	4.3	2.1
40-49.99	29.3	27.9	35.8	14.1
50-59.99	8.4	21.9	47.5	37.3
60-69.99	.8	10.9	9.9	29.3
70-79.99	.1	4.4	1.2	11.7
80-89.99	.1	1.6	—	3.7
90-94.99	—	.3	—	1.4
No. of cases	4,368	3,305	162	676

NOTE: This table excludes (a) candidates in "free-for-all" multimember districts; (b) minor candidates or those who won less than 5% of the vote; (c) walkover candidates, those who won over 95% of the vote, many of whom had no opponent; and (d) incumbent senators opposing each other due to reapportionment.

a. *Nonmember* here refers to all candidates for the senate who are not current members of the state house.

The consequences of selectivity may also be seen by examining the percentage of the vote received by challengers for senate seats. Table 3.3 illustrates for over 8,500 contests the full 10%-interval breakdown of votes received by the challengers in "contested" elections (see table notes). The least successful are non-house members who challenge incumbents (second column). The most successful are the house members who challenge for an open seat, illustrated in the last column. House candidates do better than other candidates, and both types fare better in open elections. It is worth noting that often, when there are more than two candidates, elections are won with less than 50% of the vote, so many of those in the 40% to 50% row did win their elections.

Another way to treat the information in Table 3.3 is to ask what percentage of the vote a candidate was likely to receive. A statistical model applied to the general election data produces the following relationship:

% Vote for Senate Seat = 35.7 + 10.0 (Open Seat) + 14.3 (House Challenger)

This "regression equation" finds, as expected, that on average in "contested" senate elections in this 18-year period nonincumbents fared better in open elections and house members garnered more votes than other nonincumbent candidates.[4] *House* members who ran for an *open* seat could be expected to win about 60% of the vote, including

- The 35.7% of the vote that a non-house candidate against an incumbent would be expected to win
- The 10% additional vote if it was an open seat
- The 14.3% additional vote if the challenger was a house member

Implications

In sum, the above analysis supports the notion that legislators engage in a kind of rational selectivity in making career decisions. Senate seats are more attractive than house seats but not that much more attractive. Most house members do not attempt to move up until the odds of winning are very favorable. It is useful perhaps to contrast this kind of explanation of election success with those discussed earlier that focus upon campaign strategy, external conditions, and candidate attributes. Implicit in the rational selectivity argument is the notion that legislators take into account many of the variables normally employed in these other approaches. House members are relatively knowledgeable about what is necessary to win higher office. Many wait until they will not face a formidable opponent (i.e., an incumbent senator or another house member) and perhaps until political and economic conditions are more favorable to their success. These favorable circumstances in turn make it easier to raise the campaign funds that also facilitate success. It may not be so surprising that with this strategic behavior these house members succeed 82.8% of the time.

Now, it may be argued that with such a high success rate against incumbents (winning two-thirds of these races) it would appear that many house members erred by not challenging more incumbent senators. But state senate incumbents have more experience in the much larger senate district and normally win about 90% of their races. The above regression equation estimates that against the typical incumbent a house member will get only 50% (35.7 + 14.3) of the vote, which hardly guarantees success. Representatives have been successful in their challenges against incumbent senators because they have selectively run against the more vulnerable incumbents, not simply because they are skilled campaigners. Races against the other incumbents would be much more difficult. Moreover, if legislators have the risk aversion found in the general population, they often would avoid taking on these very risky bids for higher office. Also, for those house members who have some power in the house, the utility of serving in the senate may not exceed the utility of serving in the house.

The fact that a house member has only a 30% probability of entering an open senate race may seem particularly puzzling, given the high success rate that representatives have in open senate races. But the average senate, with 40 members, is only 36% as large as the typical house of representatives. Thus, there are typically three house members who are potential candidates for any open senate seat, and one of these generally ends up entering the senate race. Similarly, because house challengers for open seats won 87.2% of their races in general elections, they could not have faced each other very often in these open races, no more than 6.4% of the time by our calculations.[5] The selectivity in seeking state senate seats accordingly involves more than simply waiting for an open senate seat. House members wait until there is an open senate seat *and* until they appear to be the most viable representative in the district to win the senate race. Only then do they feel they have sufficiently attractive odds of success.

State Legislature to Congress Decisions

Are state legislators so successful when they challenge for Congress? The stakes are a bit higher in these contests. Bruce Robeck (1982), in a study of the 1974, 1976, 1978, and 1980 House elections, found that about 56% of state legislator challenges were for open seats, even though only about 15% of congressional contests are open seat contests (see also Banks & Kiewiet, 1989, Table 1). Using this information, we can calculate that state legislators are about 7 times more likely to challenge for an open congressional seat than against an incumbent: $7.2 = (56/15)/(44/85)$. For most state legislators, however, a seat in Congress has a much higher value (utility) than a state legislative seat, and thus the state legislators will take greater risks to win. In doing so, they will lose more often. Robeck reported that in challenging for congressional seats, state legislators won the House primary 57% of the time, and 48% of those nominated by their party won the general election;

Table 3.4   Success of State Senators and Representatives in Races for U.S. House of Representatives: 1984, 1986, 1994, and 1996 Primaries and General Elections

	% Winning House Seat	*No. of Candidates*
All elections		
All legislators	25	303
Senators	26	144
Representatives	24	159
Open-seat elections only		
All legislators	33	184
Senators	34	90
Representatives	32	94
Incumbent reelection bid		
All legislators	13	119
Senators	13	54
Representatives	12	65

on net, a state legislator who runs for the House has only a 27% chance of entering the House ($.27 = .57 \times .48$).

Table 3.4 reports more recent data for the 1984, 1986, 1994, and 1996 primaries and general elections. For states with primaries, it reports the number of state legislators who entered a House primary and their success in winning both the primary and the general election. For states relying on party conventions to select candidates, the table indicates the number of state legislator candidates in the House general election and their success.[6] The overall success rate for state legislators running for the House is 25%, very close to that found by Robeck for the previous decade. Again there is evidence that many state legislators wait for open elections. Sixty-one percent of the state legislator candidates in more recent years challenged for open seats.

We may compare those who were currently in the state house with those who were currently in the state senate when they challenged for a congressional seat. Senators do have a larger electoral base: That is, they are known to and supported by more voters. They also tend to have more experience in office and generally have won more contests. These differences would give them an edge over house members in a congressional race. On the other hand, as noted earlier, many state senators can run for Congress without losing their state senate seat. Most state senators have a 4-year term. If a bid for Congress is made with 2 years left in the term, the risk is much less, encouraging them to be less selective in entering House races.

The figures in Table 3.4 confirm that state house members, who rarely can run at midterm, are more selective than state senators in choosing to enter a congressional race. Although there are nearly three times as many state house members as there are state senators, only slightly more house members (159 versus 144) become candidates for a congressional seat. And despite the electoral advantages that senators have over house members, the success rates for the two groups are nearly identical.

Obviously, a race against another state legislator should be a much more difficult race than one facing a less experienced opponent. And indeed this appears to be the case. In Table 3.5, it can be seen that in *open* elections state legislators are nearly twice as successful if they are not running against another state legislator (47% vs. 25%). On the other hand, in elections in which they face an incumbent, the odds of success are dismally low in either situation (13%). Given the lower success when running against another state legislator, potential candidates might be expected to avoid these confrontations. Robeck reported that nearly 30% of state legislators were running against another state legislator. This head-to-head competition is more common in the recent data in Table 3.5, involving 46% of all state legislative candidates. As expected, state legislators are more willing to run against another state legislator in open races, where their odds of success are higher than in races against an incumbent House member.

U.S. House to U.S. Senate Decisions

If a member of the U.S. House of Representatives runs for the U.S. Senate, the House seat must be forfeited. This undesirable risk should make house members very selective in deciding when to challenge. Francis et al. (1994) examined 345 U.S. Senate elections spanning 30 years (1960-1988) for the 41 states that reelected at least one senator from each party during the period. A total of 106 House members decided to enter a Senate primary. It can be seen in Table 3.6 that 59 of the 106 House candidates (56%) entered an open election, even though only 94 of the 345 elections (27%) were open. Once again, legislators are showing selectivity by often waiting for an open

Table 3.5 Impact of Competition From Other State Legislators on Success in Races for U.S. House of Representatives: 1984, 1986, 1994, and 1996 Primaries and General Elections

	% Winning House Seat	*No. of Candidates*
All elections		
All legislators	25	303
No legislative opponent	27	164
Legislative opponent	23	139
Open-seat elections only		
All legislators	33	184
No legislative opponent	47	69
Legislative opponent	25	115
Incumbent reelection bid		
All legislators	13	119
No legislative opponent	13	95
Legislative opponent	13	24

NOTE: The state legislator is counted as facing another state legislator (i.e., a legislative opponent) if another state legislator was a candidate for the House seat, irrespective of party.

Table 3.6 Success of U.S. Representatives in U.S. Senate Primaries, 1960 to 1988

	% Winning Primary	*No. in Primary*
All primary elections		
No House opponent	86	83
House opponent	43	23
Open-seat elections only		
No House opponent	83	40
House opponent	42	19
Elections with incumbent seeking reelection		
No House opponent	88	43
House opponent	50	4

election. We use a multiple-variable (i.e., multivariate) probit statistical procedure to separate the effects of the different variables on the likelihood that a House member will enter a Senate primary. In that analysis, we find that an open-seat election raises the probability of entering a primary by at least 150% (from .033 to 0.083) compared to an election with an incumbent running.

Just as we expect legislators to avoid running against incumbents, we also expect legislators to avoid running against another legislator (or quality opponent) when challenging for a higher office. Avoiding other House members would greatly raise the odds of having a successful bid for the Senate. Legislators do in fact practice this avoidance pattern. It has already been shown that the low probability of state representatives' entering state senate races helps keep head-to-head clashes between state house members to a minimum. A similar phenomenon occurs in Congress.

Recall that there is a .083 probability of entering the typical open Senate race. Because there are 435 House districts for 50 states, or nearly 9 districts per state, there should not be many confrontations between House members. Accordingly, 83 of the 106 U.S. Representatives entering a Senate primary faced no opposition from another House member in the primary, and 86% of these 83 candidates won their primary. In 10 other primaries, two House members entered (possibly with nonlegislators running also), one winning in each. In one unusual primary, three House members ran unsuccessfully, losing to Republican Pete Wilson in California, then mayor of San Diego. There were only four cases of two House members facing each other in the general election for the U.S. Senate.

We have established that House members avoid races in which they will face another House member. Is the pattern of avoidance consistent with the incentives they face? We would expect House members to avoid taking on another House member in the primary if they would later face an incumbent in the general election in what would be a very difficult race. The breakdown into "open-seat" elections and "incumbency" elections in Table 3.6 is consistent with this reasoning. In the second column, it can be seen that when seats are open, 19 of the 59 challenges for Senate seats are against House opponents, but that when there is an incumbent, only 4 of 47 attempts are so ambitious as to involve facing another House member.

Furthermore, because there are more House districts in larger states, members in larger states have a greater potential problem with head-to-head races. In the probit statistical procedure, we find that a House member

Table 3.7   Head-to-Head Confrontations Between U.S. Representatives in U.S.
Senate Primaries

State	Year	Population Rank
New York	1970	1
California	1976	1
California	1982	1
California	1986	1
Texas	1984	3
Michigan	1976	8
Maryland	1986	19
Washington	1988	20
Arizona	1976	33
Hawaii	1976	40
New Hampshire	1962	45

NOTE: Population rank reflects the rank for the census year used in the allocation of House districts in that election.

running in a state with one congressional district is four more times more likely to run in a primary and is 17 times more likely to be the party's candidate in the general election than a House member running in a state like California, which has 45 districts. However, this effect is not great enough to offset the fact that confrontations tend to be more common in the more populous states. For example, California in the 1980s had 45 House members, with many Democrats or Republicans who might oppose each other in a Senate primary, and it happened twice in four races. Table 3.7 lists the few times House members opposed one another in U.S. Senate races between 1960 and 1988. A majority are from the populous states where the likelihood of confrontation is higher.

The success rate when there is no House opponent is very high under all conditions, making it seem foolhardy to face the unfavorable odds in a Senate race against a House opponent. The House opponent has a constituency within the state, a funding base, and experience in campaigning. Prior to entering primaries, there may be ample posturing or "testing the waters" by potential candidates over whether to enter a race, but such activity does not carry over very often into campaign battles between legislators attempting to move up.

Conclusion

This chapter has reviewed a variety of evidence relating to how politicians act strategically by making decisions on a selective basis to advance their political careers. Selective decision making requires an assessment of the value of various alternatives and the risks in seeking them. For the office-holder, it is a comparison of the value of the present office with the value of an office up the ladder. The comparison is informed by an assessment of the risks and the consequences of winning or losing in each situation. Because running for office can be a risky business, one might conclude that office-holders must be risk takers. It is clear, however, that most officeholders exercise considerable care, typically running for reelection rather than challenging upward against formidable odds. They tend to wait for an open election where they will not have to compete against another quality opponent with similar political experience.

In the next chapter, we will see how term limits on state legislators have changed the decision-making context in 18 states. House members should compete against each other for a senate seat more often when forced to give up their house seats, and imminent eviction also may produce more frequent competition among state house and senate members for congressional seats.

Notes

1. Accurate data were not available for Vermont and Minnesota, and Nebraska is unicameral.

2. Often all the house members in a senate district are of the same party as an incumbent senator. In these situations, challenges to the incumbent are quite uncommon.

3. The data set was selected from the state election study now carried out by the Inter-University Consortium for Political and Social Research. The file accessed contained a line of information for each candidate each time the candidate ran for office ($N > 159,000$). Primary elections were excluded mainly because they were not fully recorded at the time of this analysis. The house data were used only to determine whether there was a name match with the senate list of each state.

4. Both effects are highly significant statistically.

5. We also expect that members of the same party seldom face each other in primaries, but we will need to examine congressional data for a direct test of the proposition.

6. About 95% of our state legislators who ran in House races entered a primary. A few were substituted for the primary victor after the primary.

4

Term Limits and Their Impact on Career Choice, Turnover, and Selectivity in the States

The passage of legislative term limits by 21 states in the United States may prove to be the most significant set of events to affect political careers and legislative institutions in the past 50 years.[1] Had it not been for court invalidation of their application to Congress, the consequences would have been even more far-reaching. Some observers see term limits as a great opportunity for Republicans to regain control of state legislatures. Rosenthal (1996), though, saw their passage as a reversal of a long-term trend toward institutionalized legislative decision making. *Institutionalization* is a term that was introduced over 30 years ago by Polsby (1968) in a landmark article on the U.S. House of Representatives. A legislature institutionalizes when, among other features, it increases the complexity and support (e.g., staffing) of committee operations, develops career paths within its chambers, and develops ways of insulating the members from external forces such as election challenges. These three features tend to enhance careerism in legislatures. Rosenthal argued that with regard to institutionalization, the state legislatures had been moving in the same direction as the U.S. House but that recently there had been a reversal. Term limit laws highlight the "deinstitu-tionalization" of legislatures in many states.

Careerism

Careers within legislative chambers are made possible in a number of ways. For example, it makes sense to allow members to advance to more responsible positions as they gain experience in and knowledge about legis-lative business. Such advancement can be routinized by giving only experi-enced members committee chair or vice-chair assignments and giving only proven members with long experience the chairs of all-important committees such as Appropriations or Finance. In addition, long-term members may become one of the lower-chamber party officers before becoming Speaker or Majority Leader. In her analysis of Speaker careers, Freeman (1995) found that from 1975 to 1991, state house speakers' legislative experience increased from a mean of 4.4 years to 7.8 years prior to obtaining the office. She also found that by 1991 almost all speakers had been a committee chair and that over one-third had been an assistant leader.

Political careers are more desirable and easier to plan and fulfill when legislators can resist election defeat. One way to avoid defeat is for members to vote new perks to go with the office. Such perks may include a larger staff, subsidized travel to the home district, mailing expenses, and certain other expenditures that may help legislators gain more name recognition. Legisla-tors may also vote themselves higher salaries or more generous per diem expenses to make it less necessary to find other sources of income. This allows more time to be spent on campaign matters and publicity. Also, members are simply more likely to want to be reelected if the benefits of holding office are generous.

The incentives produce a kind of careerism-perks growth spiral. The more perks there are, the more members want a career. The more members want a career, the more they wish to vote for more perks. Voting for more perks stimulates even further a greater desire for a career, and so on. But term limits can act as a spiral-smasher. They preclude a career in the chamber, which reduces the benefit from relying on perks to build a safe seat. Party leaders cannot build long-term coalitions either, so career paths in the chamber are not only shorter but also less predictable. As a result, legislators may seek out alternative offices or careers.

Term Limit Background

The earliest states to act, California, Colorado, and Oklahoma, adopted legislative term limits in 1990. Members of the lower chambers were limited to 6 years in California and 8 in Colorado, and the upper chambers were given 8-year limits. Oklahoma adopted 12-year limits for total service in the legislature. An additional 12 states passed term limits in 1992, with several imposing 6-year limits on house members (Arkansas, Michigan, Montana, Oregon, Washington, and Wyoming), and the others imposing 8-year limits (Arizona, Florida, Missouri, Ohio, and South Dakota). In all but Wyoming, the state senates were given 8-year limits. One year later, Maine passed a retroactive term limit provision that began precluding some reelection bids in 1996.

By 1994, enthusiasm for short-term limits had subsided somewhat. New term limit laws had more lenient 8- and 12-year limits, not 6-year limits, and only four states passed limits. Idaho and Massachusetts set 8-year limits for both chambers, and Nevada and Utah opted for 12-year limits for both. In 1995, Louisiana passed 12-year limits for both chambers. Louisiana was the first state without a constitutional "initiative" provision to pass limits. In 1996, not a single state enacted term limits. In fact, the state supreme court overturned the Nebraska term limit law. Later, in 1997 and 1998, Massachusetts and Washington, respectively, also encountered court reversals, leaving 18 states with term limits.

Term limits have been virtually a *voter initiative* phenomenon. Table 4.1 describes the 23 states with voter initiative provisions, listing when voter initiatives and term limits were approved and the term limits imposed on each chamber of the legislature. Most voter initiatives were established at the turn of the century during the Progressive era. Of the 23 states with voter initiatives, only Alaska, Illinois, and North Dakota have not yet imposed term limits on state legislators. These would appear to be the most likely states to enact term limits in the future, given that legislators rarely impose limits on themselves.

Term limits thus appear to result partly from voter discontent. If advocates of term limits have an easier time getting their views placed on a statewide ballot, they tend to ask for more stringent term limits. Table 4.2 summarizes term limit features for three groups of states: those with easy voter initiatives (2-8% signature requirements), those with difficult voter initiatives (10-15% signature requirements), and the one term limit state with no voter initiative

Table 4.1   Relationship Between Voter Initiative Provisions and Legislative
Term Limits

	Voter Initiatives		Legislative Term Limits		
				Years Allowed	
	Year Introduced	Signatures Required (%)	Year Passed	House	Senate
North Dakota	1914	2	—		
California	1911	5	1990	6	8
Colorado	1910	5	1990	8	8
Massachusetts	1918	5	1994[a]	8	8
Missouri	1908	5	1992	8	8
Montana	1906	5	1992	6	8
South Dakota	1898	5	1992	8	8
Ohio	1912	6	1992	8	8
Oregon	1902	6	1992	6	8
Nebraska	1912	7	1992[a]		8
Arkansas	1909	8	1992	6	8
Florida	1978	8	1992	8	8
Illinois	1970	8	—		
Michigan	1908	8	1992	6	8
Oklahoma	1907	8	1990	12[b]	12[b]
Washington	1912	8	1992[a]	6	8
Alaska	1959	10	—		
Arizona	1910	10	1992	8	8
Idaho	1912	10	1994	8	8
Maine	1908	10	1993	8	8
Nevada	1904	10	1994	12	12
Utah	1900	10	1994	12	12
Wyoming	1968	15	1992	6	12

NOTE: Louisiana is the only state with term limits (12 years for each chamber) and no initiative; it is not included in this table.

a. Reversed by state supreme court: 1996 in Nebraska, 1997 in Massachusetts, and 1998 in Washington.

b. Maximum years in both chambers combined.

(Louisiana). Term limits generally were approved first in the states with low signature requirements, then in the states with higher signature requirements, and last in a state that had no voter initiative. Furthermore, the limits were most severe in the states in which voters had the easiest time getting a voter

Table 4.2   Effect of Signature Requirements in Voter Initiative States on
Term Limits

	Voter Initiative States: Signature Requirement		
	2%-8%	10%-15%	No Voter Initiative
Number of states	13	6	1
Average year approved	1991.8	1993.2	1995
Average limit on house	7.0	9.0	12
Average limit on senate	8.0	10.0	12

NOTE: Oklahoma is not included because its restriction applies to total years served in both chambers. The term limit on the only legislative chamber in Nebraska is treated as a limit on a senate.

initiative on the ballot. Term limits were an average of 2 years shorter in the low-signature-requirement states than in the high-signature-requirement states, which in turn were 2 to 3 years shorter than in the no-voter-initiative state. The only term limit states to allow senators 12 years in office were Louisiana and half of the initiative states with a 10% or 15% signature requirement.

Before term limits were enacted, state legislators across the country were seldom defeated in reelection bids. Incumbents were estimated by Garand (1991), for example, to be successful 92% of the time they ran (p. 15; see also Jewell & Breaux, 1988).[2] Essentially, members could plan to hold the office continuously. The early conventional view of the impact of term limits was that limits merely remove legislators after a few years if they have not left sooner for the typical reasons, such as election defeat, the lure of another position, poor health, burnout, or advancing age. In reality, term limits have a much greater effect.

With sharply curtailed career options and a restriction on the number of years that the current position can be held, term limits cause legislators to *discount* the value of holding the office. For example, Daniel and Lott (1997) found that term limits in California resulted in real campaign spending falling sharply to levels experienced two decades ago. As a consequence also, other career opportunities will appear relatively more attractive. The changing conditions lead to a "churning effect." Members will anticipate the deadlines and leave office prior to the legal limits, producing a shorter tenure cycle than the laws require. If a legislator does wait until the deadline, he or she may face, unfortunately, an incumbent. Thus, it appears rational to try for an open seat earlier if one becomes available.

It seems evident that the level of turnover will increase substantially when the term limit deadlines are reached. That is, members will leave office for all of the normal reasons that caused them to exit in the past—election defeat, high opportunity costs, pursuit of higher office, advancing age, poor health, and so forth—and then term limits will sweep out those who remain. Moncrief et al. (1992) and Opheim (1994), for example, estimated the extent of these "direct" effects, the former study for a 12-year limit and the latter for an 8-year limit. The question they posed is: If term limits had been in effect over the previous, say, 8 years, how many legislators would still be in office and thus would have been booted out by term limits? For the 15 states that had term limits when Opheim wrote, almost half (48.5%) of the house members and two-thirds of the senate members (64.3%) from the class of 1985-86 would have been knocked out by term limits. The results were quite similar for states without term limits (had they imposed them). Although Opheim's results are hypothetical, the main point is clear: A major proportion of the legislative membership, between one-half and two-thirds, will be affected by 8-year term limits. But these estimates will be too low if term limits cause legislators to seek other positions before the term limit forces them from office.

Now that the clock has been ticking and deadlines are approaching, we indeed find that legislators do not necessarily wait for the deadlines to arrive. In fact, we find that members in term limit states have increased their rate of exit before term limits force the first legislators from office. We can detect this tendency by examining the turnover rates before and after term limits were enacted for both types of states, term limit states and non-term-limit states.

The Churning of Membership[3]

House elections, usually held every 2 years, give us a better database than senate elections, which are typically held every 4 years.[4] Thus, in examining the impact of term limits, we focus on *house* turnover and take account of senate turnover only as it may affect house turnover. We begin by establishing a *baseline,* which is the mean turnover rate in each state house for the years prior to the passage of the first term limits, from 1980 to 1990 or from 1982 to 1992. This span of 10 years includes a minimum of three elections and at least one reapportionment year. Most state houses had five elections, but four states elect house members only every 4 years. Also, redistricting tends to produce higher turnover, so to have comparable state data, one such year is included for each state. The median state house, for example, had a turnover rate of 23.6%. Having established such a baseline, we can determine how much turnover increased in term limit states versus non-term-limit states.

Measuring the Change

To measure the change, we compare the baseline turnover rate in each state house (Baseline) with the subsequent turnover in 1994 (or in 1996). The increase or decrease in turnover from the earlier baseline period to the later years, 1994 or 1996, where Δ signifies change, equals

$$\text{For 1994: } \Delta \text{ Turnover} = \text{Turnover94} - \text{Baseline}$$

$$\text{For 1996: } \Delta \text{ Turnover} = \text{Turnover96} - \text{Baseline}$$

Measuring the Impact

We would expect to find a greater increase in turnover in the term limit states. Why? Because *the imposition of term limits will induce many legislators to exit before the first deadline is reached.* Term limits will cause many legislators to reevaluate their career prospects and to be less selective when they evaluate bids for higher office, local office, lobbying positions, administrative appointments, and private sector opportunities. A long and continuous career in the house is no longer possible.

Though we would expect to find a *greater increase in turnover in the term limit states* in 1994 and in 1996, we would expect the effects to be even more evident as the deadlines approach. A very generous term limit of, say, 12 years, may have little if any immediate effect on career decisions. It is only later, when members are within a few years of the limit, that we should see an impact. Thus, in measuring the impact of term limits, we need to take into account how soon the first limit will be reached. And we cannot assume that the effect on turnover is linear. It seems plausible that the effect of diminishing time does grow as the binding date draws near. We estimated several different statistical models to ascertain the impact of how much time remains before the term limit first becomes binding. The most revealing model tests for the separate effects of 2 years remaining and 4 years remaining. Almost all of the early exiting caused by term limits takes place 2 years or 4 years before the deadline is reached.

Senate Exiting Effects

Even before the onslaught of term limit laws, a prominent reason for leaving state legislative office was to run for higher office. About one-third of those who left voluntarily did so to run for another office. Furthermore, most who left to run for higher office acted with great selectivity, usually running for an open seat, and house members had only a .3 probability of entering an open senate race. As a result, legislators in the lower chambers were successful in running for state senate seats almost 80% of the time (see Chapter 3). We expect that this pattern continues in the non-term-limit states; that is, house members run for senate seats infrequently but are highly successful when they do.

In term limit states, there is an even greater incentive to take advantage of open senate seats. A race for an open senate seat this year may be more successful than a race against a senate incumbent later, when the term limit prevents the representative from seeking reelection.

Thus, an increase in the number of available senate seats should result in greater house turnover. House members know when a senator is leaving office voluntarily and can respond by running for that senate seat. Senate opportunities are measured by the exit rate in the senate, excluding election defeats, for the same year. Note that in the target years, 1994 and 1996, it is unlikely that a major proportion of senate vacancies were caused by term limits because they tended to be as long or longer than the house, either 8 or 12 years. Even so, the normal vacating of senate seats should be positively related to house turnover.

Competing Explanations

In a scientific study, the cause-and-effect connection between term limits and increased early turnover must be established in part by taking into account other possible explanations. In this case, we control for changes in turnover due to other factors, including (a) changes in the professionalization of the legislatures between the 1980s and 1990s, (b) the Republican surge of 1994, (c) intrastate partisan shifts, and (d) past turnover levels.

Professionalization

State legislatures are often compared with one another on the basis of how professionalized they have become. A highly "professionalized" legislature offers high pay and generous staff support to its members and requires long legislative sessions. An amateur legislature, in contrast, offers low pay and little staff support and meets for only a short time during the year. Congress would be a model of a highly professionalized legislature. But California and New York would rank high also. Squire (1992) rated the professionalization of each state legislature according to how close each came to Congress on a combination of the three elements: compensation, length of session, and staff support. Those in highly professionalized legislatures find other positions less attractive, and legislative turnover has been found to be lower in these states (Squire, 1988). Accordingly, changes in professionalization between the 1980s and the 1990s should affect changes in turnover. We use King's (1997) measures based on the Squire system for each decade to control for professionalization changes.

The Republican Surge

In 1994, the Republicans were enjoying an upswing in support, reflected not only in congressional elections but also in state legislative elections across the country. The Republican nationwide surge in 1994, due to a variety of factors, including a lack of Democratic cohesion at the national level and superb Republican party campaign organization, may have had a significant impact on turnover. To tap into the potential for such an effect, the party distribution of seats before the elections occurred needs to be determined. The Republican surge should have produced the greatest turnover in states that were dominated by Democrats. To take the extreme for illustration purposes, if a state had 90% Republican seats, there could not have been much of a surge in seat advantage, but if the Democrats had 90% of the seats, there was great potential. We hypothesize that *in 1994, there was greater turnover in legislative chambers, with a higher percentage of Democrats in the previous term.* The 1996 elections, however, allowed Democrats to regain some ground, and we would not expect the same effect of the percentage of legislators who were Democrats.

It is also important to control for the party composition of the state legislature because there were substantial differences between the two parties in support for term limits. Republicans tended to support term limits, and Democrats tended to oppose them. The "Contract With America" platform voiced by the U.S. House Republicans in 1994, for example, contained a term limit plank. There is reason to believe that the Republicans instigated or at least jumped on the term limit bandwagon to help move their party from minority to majority status.[5]

Intrastate Party Shifts

As noted above, some legislative turnover is due to the shifting fortunes of the two parties in the state. A gain by one party is reflected in a loss of seats by the other party. And the national trends discussed previously do not capture the changing fortunes of all the state parties. It is possible that those states with term limits were experiencing major shifts in partisan control, creating higher legislative turnover, and that our expected term limit effects would disappear when such shifts were taken into account. We measure these shifts in state party strength by the fraction of seats gained that year by the successful party in the state.

The Baseline

States with very low turnover in the baseline years have much greater potential for turnover to increase later, with or without term limits. The potential for legislative turnover in California to increase dramatically in the 1990s is much greater than in, say, Wyoming, where the turnover before term limits was much higher in the 1980s (see Table 4.5, Column 1). States with high turnover initially are expected to have less of an increase in subsequent years. Thus, in attempting to explain changes in turnover, we need to control for the base rate in each state during the 1980 to 1990 period. We would not want to attribute changes in turnover to term limits if the changes were simply a reflection of how low the turnover had been during the baseline period.

Table 4.3   Variables Affecting Turnover Prior to Term Limit Deadlines

Variable Description	Regression Coefficient b	Significance Value t	Probability Value p <
1. Two years left until deadline	.069	3.40	.001
2. Four years left until deadline	.031	1.79*	.094
3. Voluntary exiting in senate	.327	4.73	.001
4. Change in professionalization of legislature	−.140	−1.54	.129
5. Percentage incumbent Democrats before election	.382	3.39	.001
6. Year: coded 2 for 1996 and 1 for 1994	.094	2.28	.026
7. Interaction term: (percentage Democrats × year)	−.212	−2.98	.004
8. Level of turnover during baseline years	−.511	−5.16	.001
9. Percentage party shift in seats in state house	.664	4.65	.001

NOTE: Intercept = −.172. Adjusted R^2 = .55; N = 88.
*Significant at 5% level for one-tailed test only.

Results

We test these hypotheses using turnover data from the 1994 and 1996 elections. Because we are examining the impact of term limits before they become binding, our data for 1996 exclude California and Maine, where term limits precluded some house members from seeking reelection.[6] A statistical analysis of the above factors, reported in Table 4.3, suggests that most, if not all, of the above explanations have some merit. That is, each of these factors accounts for part of the change in turnover between the baseline period and 1994 or 1996. The negative coefficient on the baseline turnover rate indicates that turnover increased in states that had a low baseline turnover rate and decreased in states with a high initial turnover rate. Heavily Democratic chambers experienced a marked increase in turnover in 1994 when the Republicans gained control of Congress and a small decrease in 1996 when the Democrats regained some ground.[7] Similarly, the positive coefficient on percent party shift in seats in state house implies that turnover increased more in states that had a greater shift in party control of the house. There is also some weak statistical evidence (even with a one-tailed test) that turnover decreased in legislatures that became more professionalized in the 1990s.

Let us now turn to the crucial term limit and senate turnover effects on house turnover. The evidence in Table 4.3 confirms that term limit laws did indeed lead to higher turnover even prior to the first term limit deadlines. The first two regression coefficients (*b*) indicate that

1. There is a 6.9% greater turnover (i.e., from 23.6% to 30.5%) when only 2 years are left until the first deadline, compared to when there are 6 or more years left.
2. There is a 3.1% greater turnover when only 4 years are left until the deadline, compared to when there are 6 or more years left.

As expected, states with more "voluntary" turnover in the senate experienced an increase in house turnover. The regression coefficient (*b*) implies that for every 1% increase in "voluntary" senate turnover, there is an 0.327% increase in house turnover. This estimate seems reasonable given that the average senate has about 40 members, or 36% of the average size of state houses. It is consistent with our 1993 estimate, based on different data, that there was about a 0.3 probability that house members would run for an open senate seat. We may note that senators in Maine in 1994 and California in 1996 were only 2 years from their limit deadlines. Total senate turnover in these cases averaged almost 17% higher than turnover during the 10-year baseline period, which will be reported in Table 4.5. The regression coefficient in Table 4.3 implies that this increase in senate turnover due to term limits produces a sizeable impact on house turnover rates. So term limits result in both a direct and indirect effect, the latter due to rising senate turnover.

Challenges for U.S. House Seats

The higher turnover in state legislatures should result in more quality candidates challenging at the next level, and thus more competitive races. State house members are led to enter more state senate and U.S. House races, and state senators are increasingly likely to run for Congress. There is evidence that term limits have led many more state legislators to challenge for a seat in the U.S. House, even before term limits became binding in the state legislatures. Table 4.4 examines the change in the number of state legislative candidates in primaries and/or general elections seeking U.S. House seats in the term limit states.

Table 4.4   Early Effect of Term Limits on State Legislator Entry Into
U.S. House Races

	Annual No. of Candidates Averaged for 1984 and 1986	No. of Candidates: 1994 or 1996
	4 years until limits binding	
Senate	3.0	4
1994: CA		
1996: AZ, CO, SD		
House	3.5	10
1994: AR, CO, MI, MT, OR, WA, WY		
1996: AZ, FL, MO, OH, SD		
	2 years until limits binding	
Senate	0.5	4
1994: ME		
1996: CA		
House	4.5	10
1994: ME, CA		
1996: AR, CO, MI, MT, OR, WA, WY		

NOTE: There was no change in the number of House seats between the 1980s and the 1990s in the 12 states with 4 years until a binding term limit (Row 2). In the 9 states with 2 years until a binding limit (Row 4), the number of House seats increased from 91 to 96 over this decade.

In the first row are data for state senates in four states (one in 1994 and three in 1996) that were 4 years from term limit deadlines. In 1984 and 1986, the senates in these states produced a total of three candidates for Congress in a typical year. A decade later and still 4 years from a term limit deadline, the number of candidates increased to four. The second row similarly shows that the number of candidates from 12 state houses for a seat in the U.S. House increased dramatically from 3.5 to 10 when a term limit constraint was 4 years away.

The second two rows demonstrate the effect of facing removal from office by term limits in 2 years. The number of candidates from the California and

Maine state senates rose from 0.5 to 4, eight times its initial value. A term limit deadline 2 years away also evoked a substantial increase in candidates from state houses. In nine states in this situation, the number of candidates rose from 4.5 to 10.

Effects on Legislator Characteristics

It is fair to ask whether the churning effect noted in 1994 and 1996 will continue in evidence once all members in the chamber are elected knowing that there is a term limit. Will the new group arrive with an attitude that leads them to serve out the full term? Or will the new members see legislative service as a stepping-stone to new and better positions in the public and private sectors, pretty much in the same proportions as their predecessors who were the first to face the limits? In one respect, exiting may be greater in this earlier period. The longer experience in state politics of those in office at the time of enactment may make it easier for them to locate desirable positions elsewhere, say, as lobbyists, administrators, or consultants. In later years, when term limits have cleared out the "old" members, the new group will have less experience and fewer contacts and perhaps will not be able to move as easily to other positions. Carey, Niemi, and Powell (1998) surveyed "old-timers" and "newcomers" in the term limit states and found between them very little difference in demographic composition. We will need to wait, however, until the newcomers near their deadlines to determine whether there will continue to be churning effects. Legislators, in any case, will need to make rational career decisions in light of the available and prospective opportunities, and when the term limit deadlines are only 2 years away, the newcomers may find better opportunities.

Projecting Into the Future

The previous analysis illustrates that legislators anticipate term limit deadlines by leaving early if a good opportunity arises. One of the most attractive opportunities would be a vacated seat at the next level up. Thus, a state house member might seek an open state senate seat, or a state senator might seek an open congressional seat. Under term limit legislation, house members in the states do not need to wait very long before the seat in the senate chamber opens up. That is, once the initial stages leading up to the first term limit deadlines have passed, senate seats will begin to open up. Thus, for state house members, we have not only an office that cannot be held continuously but also new incentives in the form of open senate seats.

Direct Effects

Long-term estimates have been made to illustrate the likely impact of term limits. If we return to an earlier assumption that members will leave office for all the typical reasons for exiting in the past and that term limits will simply sweep out those who have not left by the time the deadline arrives, we can arrive at an equilibrium solution (Francis & Kenny, 1997) that produces the following projection formulas:

$$\text{6-Year Limit: } T = 1/(3 - 3B + B^2)$$
$$\text{8-Year Limit: } T = 1/[4 - 6B + 4(B^2 + B^3)]$$

where T is the projected turnover rate and B is the baseline turnover rate calculated for 1980 to 1990 (or 1982 to 1992).

Using these formulas, we are able to construct Table 4.5, which contains projections for all states, had they passed 6- or 8-year limits. The first two columns illustrate the turnover rate in the baseline period for the state houses and senates. California, for example, had turnover rates of 16.2% and 11.6% for the state house and senate respectively during the baseline period. Because the California house had 6-year limits, we use the first formula above:

$$T = 1/[3 - 3(.162) + (.162)^2] = 1/(3 - .486 + .026) = 1/2.54 = .394$$

The projected turnover rate is 39.4% (see next-to-last column in Table 4.5). The senate in California has 8-year limits, so we use the second formula above, yielding a projected turnover rate of 29.8% (see fourth column). The median estimated house turnover rates are .358 under 8-year limits and .426 under 6-year limits, which are 52% and 81% greater, respectively, than the .236 median turnover rate observed before term limits.

Table 4.5   Estimates of State House Turnover With 6- and 8-Year Term Limits
Based on Past Attrition Rates: Direct Effects and Maximum Total Effects

State	1982-1990, 1992 Attrition		8-Year Limit Direct Effect		8-Year Limit Maximum Effect	6-Year Limit Direct Effect	6-Year Limit Maximum Effect
	House	Senate	House	Senate	House	House	House
Alabama	.350	.313	.426	.403	.634	.483	.668
Alaska	.386	.240	.450	.360	.624	.502	.657
Arizona	.250	.230	.366[a]	.355[a]	.567[a]	.432	.609
Arkansas	.144	.148	.311	.313	.500	.386[a]	.552[a]
California	.162	.116	.320	.298	.496	.394[a]	.548[a]
Colorado	.306	.234	.398[a]	.357[a]	.587[a]	.460	.628
Connecticut	.242	.302	.361	.396	.591	.429	.632
Delaware	.150	.098	.314	.290	.486	.389	.539
Florida	.218	.208	.348[a]	.343[a]	.547[a]	.418	.592
Georgia	.180	.180	.329	.329	.524	.401	.572
Hawaii	.242	.178	.361	.328	.545	.429	.590
Idaho	.265	.255	.374[a]	.369[a]	.581[a]	.440	.622
Illinois	.148	.136	.313	.307	.516	.388	.565
Indiana	.170	.156	.324	.317	.512	.397	.562
Iowa	.218	.180	.348	.329	.537	.418	.583
Kansas	.214	.222	.346	.350	.550	.416	.596
Kentucky	.183	.205[b]	.330	.341[b]	.534	.402	.582
Louisiana[c]	.150	.160	.314	c	c	c	c
Maine	.254	.260	.368[a]	.371[a]	.579[a]	.434	.620
Maryland	.300	.273	.395	.379	.601	.457	.639
Massachusetts	.168	.192	.323	.335	.524	.396	.573
Michigan	.202	.297	.340	.392	.576	.411[a]	.619[a]
Minnesota	.216	.247	.347	.364	.561	.417	.605
Mississippi	.157	.193	.317	.335	.521	.391	.570
Missouri	.198	.130	.338[a]	.304[a]	.513[a]	.409	.562
Montana	.298	.232	.394	.356	.585	.457[a]	.625[a]
Nebraska	—	.212		.345			

Table 4.5   Continued

State	1982-1990, 1992 Attrition		8-Year Limit Direct Effect		8-Year Limit Maximum Effect	6-Year Limit Direct Effect	6-Year Limit Maximum Effect
	House	Senate	House	Senate	House	House	House
Nevada[c]	.350	.230	c	c	c	c	c
New Hampshire	.368	.292	.438	.390	.634	.492	.667
New Jersey	.250	.193	.366	.335	.560	.432	.604
New Mexico	.236[b]	.170	.358[b]	.324	.540	.426[b]	.586
New York	.146	.116	.312	.298	.490	.387	.543
North Carolina	.252	.268	.367	.376	.581	.433	.623
North Dakota	.280	.173	.383	.325	.557	.447	.601
Ohio	.166	.174	.322[a]	.326[a]	.517[a]	.395	.567
Oklahoma[c]	.280	.208	c	c	c	c	c
Oregon	.254	.200	.368	.339	.557	.434[a]	.601[a]
Pennsylvania	.134	.108	.306	.294	.484	.382	.537
Rhode Island	.208	.236	.343	.358	.554	.413	.599
South Carolina	.206	.214	.342	.346	.545	.412	.591
South Dakota	.278	.274	.382[a]	.379[a]	.593[a]	.446	.632
Tennessee	.180	.156	.329	.317	.515	.401	.565
Texas	.230	.192	.355	.335	.545	.423	.591
Utah[c]	.308	.206[b]	c	c	c	c	c
Vermont	.276	.294	.381	.392	.600	.445	.639
Virginia	.188	.143	.332	.311	.514	.404	.563
Washington	.274	.156	.379	.317	.550	.444	.594
West Virginia	.396	.266	.457	.375	.637	.508	.669
Wisconsin	.228	.204	.354	.341	.549	.422	.594
Wyoming	.238	.226	.359	c	c	.427[a]	c

a. Six- or eight-year term limits are in effect for these house chambers.
b. Median value.
c. Twelve-year limits. Senate only in Wyoming. Twelve years total service in Oklahoma.
From Francis and Kenny (1997). Used with permission from University of Texas Press.

Indirect and Direct Effects

It is important to note that these are long-term projections and that they do not take into account either a depreciation in the value of office or, in the case of the house, the effects of new open seats in the senate and of changes in how representatives respond to those openings. Before term limits, only 30% of house members would enter an open senate race. The desire to avoid facing an incumbent in a senate race when term limits force the representative out of the house will lead more house members to enter open senate races. Similarly, the decline in the value of the office will produce higher pre-eviction turnover as house members take advantage of other job opportunities that arise.

Columns 5 and 7 in Table 4.5 give estimates of the maximum turnover rates in the state houses, assuming that members under term limits always attempt to run for an open senate seat (see Francis & Kenny, 1997). Turnover under this assumption is enormous. Under an 8-year term limit, the median turnover rate is .549, an increase of 133% over pre-term-limit turnover. The median turnover rate under a 6-year term limit is .594, which represents an even more substantial rise in turnover.

These estimates of turnover will be too high if house members do not enter every open senate race and other sources of house turnover do not change. Two years may not be sufficient for a new representative to develop the skills and favorable reputation with the voters to make a race for the senate at all viable. The evidence in the previous section suggests, in fact, that term limits do not affect the turnover of representatives who have been only one term in the house. Thus, turnover may not reach the maximum estimates reported in Table 4.5. On the other hand, our finding that term limits increase turnover 2 to 4 years before they become binding means that the direct effect estimates are too low. The truth probably lies somewhere between the projected direct effects estimate and the maximum total effects estimate.

Term Limit Effects on the Political Career "Lottery"

In a sense, the choices encountered in a political career resemble a lottery. People who enter a common state lottery take into account the size of the plum and the probability of winning it. Political aspirants see political offices in a similar way. Of what value is the office, and what is my probability of winning it? Decisions in a political career could be seen as an assessment of these future outcomes, which involve uncertainty and risk. If the assessment is pessimistic, legislators may opt out of the election lottery and pursue another career. Potential legislators may make similar decisions.

Every 2 to 6 years, a state or national legislator is faced with a decision to select from a set of alternatives, which may include running for higher office, running for reelection, and/or returning to the local level or non-elective status. The choice available to the legislator depends on the office he or she holds and other specific conditions. The following situations are common:

1. *Minimal-Risk Choice.* A legislator may choose to run for higher office at midterm without giving up the seat that he or she holds. This situation is available primarily to senators who serve more than a 2-year term and serve in states where the practice is allowed.

2. *Multiple-Option Choice.* A legislator may choose between running for higher office, running for the same office, or returning to local elected office or nonelective status.

3. *Status Quo Choice.* A legislator may choose between running for the same office or returning to local elected office or nonelective status. This situation occurs when a higher office is not available. This would be common for members of the U.S. House, say, when a U.S. Senate seat is not open.

4. *Up-or-Out Choice (New).* A legislator may choose between running for higher office or returning to a local elected office or nonelective status because running for reelection is precluded by term limits.

These are "state-of-the-world" choices that confront officeholders. The most desirable situation from the point of view of the officeholder is the minimal-risk choice, where members do not need to relinquish their seats to run for higher office. The next most desirable situation is the multiple-option choice situation, where members must risk their own seats to run for higher office; if the risk is too high, they may decide to run for reelection. A third somewhat less desirable situation offers the status quo choice, where members can run for reelection but have no higher office up for election that year. The least desirable situation, the *up-or-out choice,* now exists for state legislators subject to term limits. Term limits reduce the value placed on a legislative career by replacing desirable situations with the least desirable up-or-out choice situation.

Under term limits, there will be fewer incumbent-versus-novice elections for two reasons. Incumbents must vacate their office, creating novice-versus-novice elections in state house races. And more members will take their experience and challenge upward, creating competition for the higher offices. Daniel and Lott (1997) did confirm that the legislative races in California have become more competitive, with fewer unchallenged seats and closer elections. Their results were supported by Petracca and O'Brien's (1996) finding that term limits on city council members led to higher voter turnout, which typically is associated with closer elections.

Most incentive structures encourage some while discouraging others. Who is encouraged under term limits? If term limits were applied to the state legislatures and Congress, a political career could advance very quickly, taking advantage of the open seats that must occur at the next highest level. A risk-prone political actor, for example, would not be held back very long by entrenched incumbents. A candidate with lifetime financial resources or occupational security might also gain by the increased open-seat opportunities. Previous studies have shown that risk-prone candidates and candidates of wealth, even before term limits existed, were more likely to challenge upward (Brace, 1984; Francis et al., 1994; Rohde, 1979). With term limits applied only to the states, members of those states with political ambition can rise to the state senate rather quickly, not having to wait for an incumbent to retire.

Term Limits Versus the Electoral Mechanism

The traditional solution to poor performance in office is for citizens to vote legislators or chief executives out of office. But for many offices, voters have difficulty perceiving who, for example, has become responsive only to special interests at the cost of the larger majority. That is, voters may have difficulty perceiving whether their representative is casting the votes they would like cast. Incumbents have clear information advantages. They can send out a stream of positive messages during their term and can command greater campaign resources to offset negative information from challengers. A citizen would need to be very attentive to public affairs to objectively monitor the representative's official behavior.

The alternative course of action for the voter is to enact term limits. Such an alternative is costly in part because experienced officials are often replaced with novices. Under term limits, the most experienced legislators are forced to either move up or move out. Elected officials, like other workers, learn on the job and thus become more skilled and knowledgeable. Replacing those who have become experts on their areas of specialization with newly elected officials who know little can lead to poorly informed decisions, especially in a complex government. For example, when Sam Nunn was in the U.S. Senate, his very informed opinions on defense issues commanded a great deal of respect from both parties. He was very difficult to replace when he chose not to run for reelection in 1996, after 24 years in the Senate. Furthermore, if term limits had forced him out of office after 6 or 8 years, he would not have had the opportunity to fully develop the expertise for which he became so renowned.

Opponents of term limits point out another hazard. Term limits produce larger numbers of members in their last or so-called "lame duck" term. With reelection to this position ruled out by term limits, officials have no incentive to satisfy the voters who put them in office (e.g., see Barro, 1973; Lott & Bronars, 1993). For example, someone who campaigned as a liberal could disappoint constituents by supporting conservative causes in the last term. Or a legislator might pay little attention to obtaining "pork" for the district and might cater to statewide rather than district interests (see Carey et al., 1998).

Will term limits on state legislatures produce much of a "lame duck" problem? Francis and Kenny (1997) estimated that for 8-year term limits the median direct turnover rate of .36 and the median total turnover rate of .55 result in a "lame duck" cohort that composes 11% and 5%, respectively, of the chamber. Consequently, there should not be too many members in their last term who have no incentive to represent their voters' interests. The downside is that there will be very few who have the maximum experience allowed by term limits.

Evidence From Gubernatorial Term Limits

In contrast to term limits for state legislatures, term limits have been in place on elected chief executives for a long time.[8] Grofman and Sutherland (1996) reported that 17 states have had term limits on governors since they were admitted to statehood.[9] The number of states with term limits has grown over time, and in 1996-97, 34 states restricted the number of terms a governor might stay in office. Term limits on mayors are less common, used in only 9 of the 47 largest cities and 7 of 97 smaller cities (Adams & Kenny, 1986).

Term limits should be more common when the electoral mechanism is less effective—say, when voters are not well informed or cannot process information very well. Adams and Kenny found that term limits were more likely (a) in rural states, where newspapers are less common and competition among television station news shows is almost nonexistent, and (b) in less educated state populations, where voters may be less adept at sorting through campaign promises (see Chapter 5). Over time, the length of the governor's term of office has been increased in many states. As a result, governors are subjected less frequently to voter scrutiny, causing a decline in the effectiveness of the electoral mechanism. This has been countered by a greater reliance on term limits. Adams and Kenny (1986) found that term limits are about 75% more likely under a 4-year term than under a 2-year term. Grofman and Sutherland (1996) reported a −.97 correlation between the mean length of gubernatorial terms and the proportion of states with a term limit, based on decennial data from 1870 to 1990.

Why Term Limits on State Legislatures?

Why have voters recently placed term limits on state legislators? It should reflect a problem that has grown over time. The answer cannot lie in legislative term length or in voter education. There have been very few changes in the last 40 years in the length of terms for the state house or senate. And educational attainment has risen, which should actually reduce the need for term limits.

The most likely explanation is associated with the rapid rise in campaign spending at all levels of government.[10] The contributions that fund these campaigns greatly favor the incumbent. Grier (1989), for example, found that incumbents in U.S. Senate campaigns raised twice the contributions of their challengers. Moncrief (1998) reported incumbent and challenger campaign expenditures for 18 states, and in 1992, for example, the median challenger expenditure was only 43% of the median incumbent expenditures. Between 1986 and 1992, the differences were greatest in California, where challengers spent only 3% to 6% of what incumbents spent. Thus, the growth of campaign spending has given incumbents a greater advantage. As Jewell and Breaux (1988, 1991) have shown for state legislative elections, incumbents running in primaries and general elections now not only win over 90% of their races but, when they win in general elections, receive on average between 70% and 80% of the vote. This deterioration of the electoral mechanism has made term limits more attractive.

Not surprisingly, the debate over term limits has followed partisan lines. Democrats have seen campaign-spending controls, an alternative to term limits, as a way of limiting the success of their wealthier Republican opponents. And Republicans have seen term limits as a way of reducing the Democratic majority to a minority. But even if the Republicans do achieve a majority in many states with the help of term limits, 6 or 8 years later, the Republican majorities will be threatened by the same term limits.

Conclusion

In conclusion, we can consider the question of what term limits will do to career incentives. As has been shown, term limits make a political career a more risky program of action. The incentives are altered to attract those with progressive political ambitions, those who are willing or able to take electoral risks. The chamber career is no longer so viable. At the other end are those who serve with the intention of returning to nonelective status, the so-called short-timers, amateurs, or citizen legislators, who serve now in ample numbers in many state legislatures and who served in much greater numbers in times past. Will term limits tip the balance in this direction? One can speculate that in states with professional state legislatures, where salaries and perks tend to be greater, quality contests will be more frequent, with "past" legislators returning to run again (as the law permits in several states) in primaries and general elections. Also, in these states the need to move up will seem more necessary to preserve a nearly full-time political career. In the more "amateur" states, where legislators serve briefly each year for very little pay, the dropout rate is likely to increase substantially. The semipermanent elected cadre who typically govern these legislative chambers will have their ranks depleted on a regular basis.

Notes

1. For excellent discussions of legislative term limits, see Grofman (1996) and Carey et al. (in press).

2. This somewhat overstates the ease with which incumbents could get reelected because some incumbents who anticipate a tough reelection race choose not to run for reelection.

3. This analysis is based on Francis et al. (1998).

4. The house turnover rates have less noise in them because they are based on more frequent elections for more seats.

5. The Democrats at the turn of the century favored the direct election of U.S. senators for the same reason. See Kenny and Rush (1990).

6. The regression used 88 observations for the 2 years. The analysis also excludes Nebraska, which has a single nonpartisan chamber.

7. The effect of % Incumbent Democrats equals .170, or $.382 - (1 \times .212)$, in 1994 and equals $-.042$, or $.382 - (2 \times .212)$, in 1996.

8. Nineteen nations in 1986 limited the number of terms their president could stay in office, and at least six others have done so in the past (Adams & Kenny, 1986).

9. They do not count interruptions during Reconstruction in the South.

10. Lott (1996) argued that campaign spending has risen because government has grown, raising the stakes in the outcome of elections. The increasing professionalization of state legislatures also could play a role because that would raise the value of legislative office.

5

Party Competition Over Policy

At the state and national levels, politicians traditionally seek reelection repeatedly until their odds of winning higher office become quite favorable—say, when they would be the frontrunner for an open seat. Term limits, of course, make such a strategy infeasible and consequently encourage legislators to risk earlier challenges for higher office, even against quality opponents. In seeking reelection, public officials will need to consider carefully the extent to which their public voting record is consistent with the preferences of their constituents. Taking liberal positions in a conservative district, for example, could make the candidate vulnerable to challenge in the next election. A loss could do serious damage to the legislator's political career. To return to this office, the loser must defeat the new incumbent, which would be difficult given the advantages incumbents have. Furthermore, the losing incumbent's lack of success in satisfying constituents may discourage potential backers in any campaign to return to political office.

Thus, an important part of political campaigns is the major struggle between candidates over policies, with each candidate claiming to do a better job of representing the voters' positions on various policy issues. Candidates who have held office have some record on which to run and for which to be criticized. Information about the actual voting record of members of

Congress is made public by various interest groups, through their ratings of how closely each legislator has adhered to the group's desires.[1] These ratings are distributed to members of their organizations and are more broadly disseminated to the media and interested voters by organizations such as Project Vote Smart.[2] The candidates' votes on specific bills and the interest group ratings provide fuel for heated political debate over policy. Even for lesser offices, as in the state legislature, interest group representatives and news media personnel keep tallies on votes cast in order to be able to report back to their members and audience.

There are two principal models of how political parties and candidates behave as they compete for voter support. According to the *median voter* model, competition for votes pulls the parties and candidates together so that they *converge* to one common central position preferred by the median voter. The *divergent platform* model, in contrast, states that parties and candidates select different positions on issues to attract the support of distinctive constituencies.

In essence, political careers are sustained in part by taking positions on policies that are consistent with constituency interests. In this chapter, we use the median voter and divergent platform models to evaluate how legislators win reelection. A dilemma occurs, however, when a member in a conservative district wishes to seek higher office in a larger liberal district or when the lesser district is liberal and the larger district is conservative. Can the legislator establish a voting record that will help to bring about a successful bid for higher office without upsetting voters in the current district? Are legislators from lesser districts that are much different from the larger district doomed to fail in any bid for higher office? In the next chapter, we test the same party competition models in assessing how members' voting records affect their ability to move to higher office.

For our purposes here, we rely on congressional evidence. Virtually all of the research on policy competition has been on the U.S. House and Senate, using one of many measures of the representatives' and senators' voting records. There are ratings of state legislators' voting records compiled by different groups in several states. The inconsistency in these ratings from state to state has greatly limited their usefulness for research comparing legislators across states; nevertheless, the analysis that we describe for Congress could be performed for a state legislature using one of the interest group ratings for that legislature.

Research on congressional voting on bills and amendments has revealed that the legislators can be located on a single voting dimension, usually referred to as a conservative-liberal dimension or right-left ideological dimension. Although in principle legislative roll call votes could reflect many different influences or "dimensions" (e.g., personal freedoms, economic policies, international involvement), the empirical reality is that a single conservative-liberal dimension appears to explain most votes cast by legislators. One commonly used measure of where members of Congress lie on this dimension is compiled by the Americans for Democratic Action (ADA). The ratings of this liberal organization range from 0 to 100, where 0 is the most conservative score and 100 is the most liberal score. Many Republican legislators vote on the conservative half of the dimension, and many Democratic legislators vote on the liberal half of the dimension (i.e., have high ADA scores).

Exactly where a member will locate on the dimension will depend in part on the member's perceptions of how liberal the central or median voter is in his or her district. In the median voter model, that is all that is relevant. In the divergent platform model, however, candidates from the same district represent different constituencies within the district and draw different citizens to the polls. The evidence reviewed in this and the next chapter favors the divergent platform model. For example, in most states, U.S. senators from different parties representing the same state have markedly different ADA scores. In Florida, for instance, Republican Senator Connie Mack and Democratic Senator Bob Graham were both elected (and reelected not many years apart) in a statewide election, yet their voting records in Congress are far from similar. In 1996, Connie Mack received an ADA score of 0, whereas Bob Graham received a score of 85. Obviously, both are not casting votes that would please Florida's median voter.

Later, we will see also that the pressures that each major political party faces in order to be viable within each state actually result in state party positions that vary greatly across the nation. Thus, nationwide, there is some ideological overlap between the parties. Southern Democrats, for example, sometimes are more conservative than Middle Atlantic or New England Republicans.

These *state* party positions play a very important role in American politics. Senators who are too liberal or conservative for their state party are unlikely to be reelected and correspondingly are less likely to seek reelection. In the next chapter, these insights will be valuable for better understanding the role of the legislator's ideological voting record in determining who moves up the political ladder. We will see that House members who are far from the state party position are much less likely to enter a Senate race and much less likely to be selected as the state party's standard bearer in the general election. Representatives who aspire to the Senate recognize the importance of establishing an appropriate voting record, for the evidence suggests that they tend to shift toward the state party position over their entire career in the House.

The Role of Retrospective Voting

Although voters may elect the candidate who promises to pursue the policies they prefer, they have no guarantee that the candidate actually will fulfill these promises once in office. For example, a liberal candidate in a conservative district could pretend to be a conservative and promise to follow conservative policies when elected. Then, once in office, he or she could support liberal bills.

Clearly, the legislator needs some incentive to follow voters' wishes. Suppose that voters reelect only those who have cast votes in favor of bills supported by a majority of voters. This is called *retrospective voting* because voters base their decisions on the incumbent's record prior to the election. Retrospective voting provides a strong incentive for the legislator to cast the votes the electorate prefers. If the legislator does not vote appropriately, the next election will be lost. A number of theoretical models have shown that retrospective voting is the best mechanism for voters to get the legislator to support the voters' preferred policies while in office.[3]

Alternatively, voters could support the candidate who they anticipate will be most likely to cast the votes that they would prefer. In this forward-looking scenario, there is *prospective voting*. That is, the electorate supports the candidate whose forecasted record for next term is closer to the voters' preferred positions.[4] Even here we can see that exactly how liberal the candidate is expected to be next term is based on how liberal he or she was during the last term. For example, a candidate who supported liberal positions in the past is expected to support liberal positions in the future. Voters look (retrospectively) to past behavior to forecast that the candidate will be a liberal. In this sense, prospective voting also involves the retrospective use of the incumbent's prior voting record. Under both retrospective and prospective voting, the electorate is expected to take account of the votes that the incumbent has cast while in office.

Policy Competition

Because there are many issues that concern voters, the competition among candidates for office can take place over many dimensions, reflecting differences over military spending, welfare programs, school quality, abortion, regulation of monopolies, and so on. In reality, however, as indicated previously, very few dimensions appear to be necessary to explain how elected officials cast votes.

Poole and Rosenthal (1997) have studied the entire history of voting in Congress. They found that a legislator's position on one dimension alone was able to explain 80.6% of the votes cast in the Senate and 82.7% of the votes cast in the House. This dimension, except for the years from 1817 to 1835 and from 1853 to 1876, was characterized by disagreement over the role of government in the economy—that is, by the struggle between what we call liberals and conservatives.[5]

The results imply that in most years the differences between members of Congress can be described as differences between liberals, moderates, and conservatives. Let us then turn to two models that explain competition among candidates along a single conservative-liberal dimension, which accounts for most position taking in Congress.

Median Voter Model

Each voter can be placed on a conservative-liberal scale that captures the full range in ideologies, from ultraconservative to moderate conservative to moderate to moderate liberal to ultraliberal. With some reasonable assumptions, it can be shown that voters will prefer the candidate whose platform is closer to their ideology or ideal position.

In Figure 5.1, the distribution of the voters' ideal positions on the conservative-liberal scale is depicted.[6] To be consistent with the empirical analysis that follows, the conservative-liberal scale on the horizontal axis assigns low numbers (i.e., on the left side of the figure) to conservatives and high numbers (i.e., on the right side of the figure) to liberals. The height of

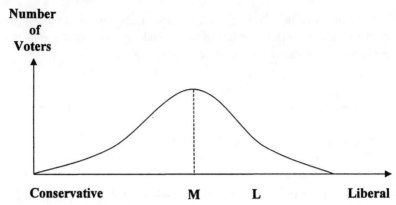

Figure 5.1. Distribution of Voters' Ideal Positions on the Conservative-Liberal Scale. *M*, median ideology; if the Democratic candidate adopts platform *L* and the Republican candidate adopts median platform *M*, the Democratic candidate will receive fewer votes.

the distribution represents the number of voters with a given ideology. The median ideology is labeled *M*. In this context, half the voters are more liberal and half are less liberal than *M*. For example, if there were 101 voters who were ordered by how liberal they were, then the median ideology would be the ideology of the 51st voter.

Suppose that the Democratic candidate chose platform *L*, which is more liberal than the median ideology. If the Republican candidate promised to follow the median ideology *M*, he could count on support from (a) voters who were more conservative than the median voter, representing one-half of the electorate, and (b) voters whose ideologies lay between *M* and the midpoint between *M* and *L* $[(M + L)/2]$. This would give him more than half the votes. Thus, a platform that differs from the median ideology always can be defeated by the platform preferred by the median voter. Candidates, realizing this, have an incentive to choose the median voter's preferred platform. There are many models of candidate competition that presume that the basic convergent forces—those that propel both candidates toward the median voter's ideological position—are at work.[7]

Divergent Platform Model

Although the median voter model often is associated with Downs' (1957) classic development of political competition, Downs recognized problems

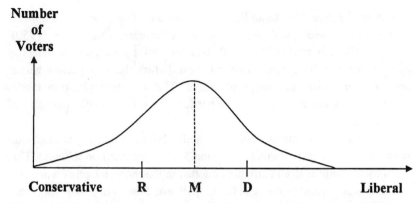

Figure 5.2. Candidate Competition Under Divergent Platforms. *M*, median ideology; *D*, platform adopted by a Democratic candidate; *R*, platform adopted by a Republican candidate (see text).

with the model's implications when he wrote, "Citizens see little point in voting if all choices are identical, so differences between platforms must be created to entice voters to the polls" (p. 98).

A variety of assumptions can lead to the conclusion that electoral competition results in candidates' choosing two distinct, divergent platforms. Fedderson (1992), in the spirit of the previous quote from Downs, proved that the cost of voting can lead to candidates staking out different positions. In Palfrey (1984), two major parties are led to select policies that are far enough apart to prevent a third party from entering and winning the election. Morton (1987) showed that some configurations of voter preferences can result in divergent platforms. In other models, candidates are driven apart by their own policy preferences, the greater influence of those constituents with extreme ideological positions, or a restriction on how much platforms can change over time. Party primaries also may play a role in creating divergent platforms.[8]

Candidate competition under divergent platforms is depicted in Figure 5.2. The Democratic candidate selects a platform *D* that is more liberal than the median ideology *M*, and the Republican candidate similarly selects a platform *R* that is more conservative than *M*. These platforms thus straddle the median voter's preferred platform. With no other considerations, each party should have an equal chance of winning the election.[9]

The candidates' different platforms give voters a reason to care who is elected. Liberals prefer to see the Democratic candidate elected, and conservatives prefer to see the Republican candidate win. Thus, each party appeals to a different ideological segment of the electorate. Huntington (1950), Fiorina (1974), Fenno (1978), and Peltzman (1984) have argued, in what has been called the "two constituencies thesis," that the two parties garner support from different groups of voters. The divergent platform model provides an explanation for why the parties have different constituencies of supporters.

In contrast, under the median voter model, both candidates promise to do what the median voter wants (e.g., spend $5,000 per pupil on schools). This leads to the empirically falsifiable conclusion that no voter cares who wins and that consequently one candidate will not fare better than the other candidate with any group. The empirical evidence is quite inconsistent with this simple prediction of the median voter model and instead supports the two constituency thesis. Jung, Kenny, and Lott (1994) examined county voting patterns in 43 states for the state's two U.S. Senate elections in 1978, 1980, or 1982.[10] Both senators, of course, are elected in a statewide race in which every registered voter in the state is eligible to vote. In 35 states, representing 81% of their states, Jung et al. found evidence that the two senators drew support from different segments of the state's population. Although pure statistical chance could produce "evidence" of different support groups (i.e., electoral coalitions) in a few states, it is clear that finding different support groups in 81% of the states is inconsistent with the median voter model.[11]

Party Differences in Roll Call Voting Record

Under the median voter model, it should not matter whether Ohio elects a Democratic or Republican senator. Both are hypothesized to support measures favored by the median voter and thus should have the same voting record in Congress. However, if the divergent platform model is correct, a Democrat from Ohio will have a more liberal voting record than a Republican from that state.

As noted previously, most disagreement in the U.S. Congress appears to be located on the conservative-liberal dimension. The ADA rating is a widely used measure of how liberal members of Congress are, relative to the other members in the chamber.[12] The organization selects a large number of roll call votes each year on which it feels that a member should cast a liberal vote.

Members are given a percentage score based on the frequency with which they take the liberal position.

Grofman, Griffin, and Glazer (1990) examined what happened to ADA scores in the U.S. Senate in 1960-1984 when a Senate seat changed parties. They found that ADA scores went up an average of 52.6 points (out of 100) when a Democrat replaced a Republican and that ADA scores fell by 32.7 points when a Democrat was followed by a Republican. Their results suggest that the two parties were 33 to 53 points apart on average.

These aggregate results mask a tremendous variation in party positions between the states. In Table 5.1, we report the average "corrected" ADA scores in the U.S. Senate by party in each state for the years 1960 to 1978 and 1979 to 1997.[13] These data provide information on how party positions in state-level competition are chosen. Three states for nearly four decades have elected senators from only one party: Kansas was exclusively Republican, and Louisiana and West Virginia sent only Democrats to the Senate. In the other 47 states, there was enough party competition to result in at least some sharing of Senate offices.

The party differences and underlying electoral competition are described much better by the divergent platform model than by the median voter model. In 78 of 83 comparisons, the ADA scores for a state's Democratic senators are significantly more liberal than those for the state's Republican senators. The only states in which the two parties did not have statistically different voting records were New Jersey, New York, and Virginia between 1960 and 1978 and Connecticut and Idaho between 1979 and 1997. New Jersey was the only state in which there was no noticeable difference between the parties for the entire 38-year period. In the years 1960 through 1978, the parties were 45 points apart in the median state and between 23 and 73 points apart in two-thirds of the states. The distance between the parties seems to have grown. In the later period, the parties were 56 points apart in the median state and between 34 and 70 points apart in two-thirds of the states.

Although it is clear that there are sharp differences between the parties, the pressures that Democrats in conservative states and Republicans in liberal states face to be viable parties in those states produce some ideological overlap. The state average ADA scores for Democrats ranged from 4 to 98 in the years 1960 through 1978 and from 33 to 99 in the years 1979 through 1997. Similarly, the average Republican ADA scores varied from 1 to 88 in the early period and from 0 to 79 in the later period. In the 1960s and 1970s, the 11 most liberal Republican state party records were more liberal than the

Table 5.1   Average ADA[a] Scores, by Party

	1960-1978			1979-1997		
	Democrat	*Republican*	*Difference*	*Democrat*	*Republican*	*Difference*
Alabama	20.0*	—	—	36.9	4.2	32.7**
Alaska	76.7	30.7*	46.7**	81.0	16.4	64.6**
Arizona	38.4*	2.9*	35.5**	57.9	7.4	50.5**
Arkansas	32.6*	—	—	74.0	0.0	74.0**
California	88.9	32.7*	56.2**	92.6	14.9	77.7**
Colorado	91.2	13.9	77.3**	86.2	11.7	74.5**
Connecticut	80.1	54.2*	25.9**	79.3	79.3	0.0
Delaware	70.0	24.1	45.9**	83.1	21.5	61.6**
Florida	26.9*	5.2	21.7**	58.7	10.0	48.7**
Georgia	12.6*	—	—	51.3	5.5	45.8**
Hawaii	77.0*	37.1	39.9**	86.1	—	—
Idaho	83.6*	8.8*	74.8**	56.5	2.4	54.1
Illinois	88.1	40.0	48.1**	78.6	45.2	33.4**
Indiana	82.2	9.6	72.6**	76.5	9.9	66.6**
Iowa	91.8	12.6	79.2**	93.3	15.4	77.9**
Kansas	—	21.3	—	—	21.0	—
Kentucky	52.4*	40.1*	12.3**	62.1	6.2	55.9**
Louisiana	21.7*	—	—	44.2	—	—
Maine	89.1	41.2	47.9**	84.1	46.5	37.6**
Maryland	83.5*	48.8*	34.7**	94.1	71.1	23.0**
Massachusetts	96.3*	63.5	32.8**	92.8	—	—
Michigan	94.7*	22.1	72.6**	91.2	11.7	79.5**
Minnesota	90.2*	—	—	99.3	34.7	64.6**
Mississippi	4.2*	—	—	33.0	7.2	25.8**
Missouri	78.6	25.0	53.6**	86.3	21.1	65.2**
Montana	80.4	—	—	76.4	6.2	70.2**
Nebraska	25.0	2.5	22.5**	50.0	1.7	48.3**

Table 5.1   Continued

	1960-1978			1979-1997		
	Democrat	Republican	Difference	Democrat	Republican	Difference
Nevada	40.3*	9.8*	30.5**	66.8	3.5	63.3**
New Hampshire	71.8	7.6	64.2**	50.5	12.0	38.5**
New Jersey	90.7	88.0*	2.7	90.6	22.0	68.6**
New Mexico	61.6*	12.1	49.5**	76.9	15.3	61.6**
New York	87.3	68.0*	19.3	85.8	29.1	56.7**
North Carolina	15.4*	2.7	12.7**	67.1	3.4	63.7**
North Dakota	79.5	6.7*	72.8**	83.5	34.9	48.6**
Ohio	65.3*	34.0*	31.3**	86.9	10.0	76.9**
Oklahoma	63.5*	14.3*	49.2**	44.6	4.2	40.4**
Oregon	92.4	64.3*	28.1**	87.5	54.9	32.6**
Pennsylvania	98.3*	53.3	45.0**	89.5	48.3	41.2**
Rhode Island	85.1	52.5	32.6**	91.0	57.0	34.0**
South Carolina	24.1*	1.1*	23.0**	55.7	5.7	50.0**
South Dakota	91.0	10.6	80.4**	86.3	14.7	71.6**
Tennessee	67.4	13.6	53.8**	71.4	11.8	59.6**
Texas	59.7	3.7	56.0**	46.9	5.0	41.9**
Utah	85.1	4.3	80.8**	—	6.0	—
Vermont	84.3	50.0*	34.3**	91.6	61.6	30.0**
Virginia	13.3*	12.0	1.3	66.2	11.2	55.0**
Washington	70.3*	—	—	83.8	28.2	55.6**
West Virginia	53.2*	—	—	71.2	—	—
Wisconsin	85.7	43.0	42.7**	81.3	12.3	69.0**
Wyoming	65.4	3.4*	62.0**	—	10.4	—

a. ADA = Americans for Democratic Action.

*Significant difference (5% level) in party's average ADA scores in two periods.

**Significant difference (5% level) between Democrat and Republican ADA scores in that period.

11 most conservative Democratic state party positions. This overlap diminished between 1979 and 1997 as the distance between the parties increased; Republican positions in only the five most liberal states were more liberal than Democratic positions in the five most conservative states. Generally, New England and Middle Atlantic Republicans have been more liberal than Southern Democrats.

The changes in party positions over time have tended to mirror the national changes. In 19 of the 24 statistically significant changes in the Democratic position, the state's senators became more liberal. Democrats in many Southern states became more liberal as the Republican party emerged in that region and took away many of the party's more conservative voters. Similarly, Senate Republicans became more conservative in 10 of the 17 significant changes in that party's state position. Most of the exceptions to these party trends seem to reflect a shift in the state's median ideology. Thus, Republicans as well as Democrats became significantly more liberal in Arizona, Maryland, and South Carolina, and both parties became noticeably more conservative in Idaho and Oklahoma.

Voter Retribution for Being Too Liberal or Conservative

The average ADA scores for a state's senators appear to reflect long-run political pressures on a senator from that state and party. But do these average ADA scores really measure state party positions that have any meaning? One obvious test is to ascertain what happens to senators who deviate far from the party average.

If the electoral respective voting mechanism works, then legislators who are too liberal or too conservative for their constituency should not be reelected. Most of the research that has tested this prediction has used a median voter model. Bond et al. (1985) found that incumbents whose voting record was distant from that predicted for them (on the basis of their districts) attracted as a consequence more experienced, better funded challengers. Other studies generally have found that legislators who were too liberal or conservative relative to a "predicted" voting record were less likely to be reelected. The "predicted" position is based on (a) the voting record of the more recently elected senator from the state, (b) the mean ideology of the state's residents, or (c) a cross-sectional regression explaining, say, the ADA scores in Congress in a particular year.[14]

Using a divergent platform approach, Schmidt et al. (1996) tested whether a senator's voting record affects reelection. Their analysis applied to the 41 states that between 1960 and 1990 satisfied a two-party competition requirement, namely that at least one senator from each party had to be reelected during the period.[15] They examined the ADA scores (corrected for absences) of the two U.S. senators serving each year in each state over the entire 31-year period.[16] Differences over time and among senators in ADA scores were explained by several variables: the political party of the senator, the national unemployment rate, U.S. and state per capita incomes, and a number of other economic or political variables. The *state-specific* regression analyses based on these variables yielded "estimated" ADA scores, one for Democrats and one for Republicans in each state for each year.[17] The authors then calculated, for Senate incumbents facing an election, the average distance (over the 6-year term of office) of the senator's ADA score from the estimated ADA score for the senator's party in the state.

The distance measure created by Schmidt et al. (1996) produces a close correspondence to the reelection decision and success of Senate incumbents in the 1962-1990 period. Eighty-five percent of the 398 incumbents ran for reelection, and of those, 81% were successful. Table 5.2 reports how both the decision to seek reelection and the rate of success in reelection were related to the distance of the senator's ADA score from the estimated state party position described previously (not controlling here for any other effects). The results are grouped according to whether the senator was (a) a party extremist—that is, a Democrat who was more liberal than the state party or a Republican who was more conservative than the state party—or (b) a party moderate—that is, a relatively conservative Democrat or a relatively liberal Republican.

Among those who seek reelection, the effect of distance from the party position on success is striking. The probability of winning reelection falls sharply and steadily as the senator's record gets farther from the estimated party position. For party extremists, the probability of success falls from .978 for those within 5 points of the state party position to .154 for those 15 or more points from the party position. Similarly, party moderates who are 0 to 5 points from the party position have a .947 probability of success, whereas moderates at least 15 points from the party position have only a .214 probability of winning. The results for party moderates are inconsistent with

Table 5.2   Relationship Between Distance to Party Position and Probability of
Senator's Running for Reelection and Winning Reelection

	Distance to Party Position	Running for Reelection		Winning Reelection	
		Frequency	Sample	Frequency	Sample
Toward	25+	.650	20	.077	13
extreme	15-25	.813	16	.231	13
positions[a]	10-15	.800	25	.750	20
	5-10	.879	58	.882	51
	0-5	.958	48	.978	46
Toward	0-5	.852	88	.947	75
moderate	5-10	.913	92	.893	84
positions[b]	10-15	.821	28	.739	23
	15-25	.533	15	.375	8
	25+	.750	8	.000	6
Total			398		339

a. Included are Democrats who are more liberal than predicted and Republicans who are more conservative than predicted.

b. Included are Democrats who are more conservative than predicted and Republicans who are more liberal than predicted.

From Schmidt, Kenny, and Morton (1996). Used with permission from Oxford University Press.

the median voter model: Under that model, moderates who are farther from the party position, and thus closer to the median ideology, are more likely to win.

Senators are expected to take into account the effect that distance from the party position has on reelection success in determining whether to seek reelection. In Table 5.2, distance has a weaker effect on running for reelection than on winning reelection. Party extremists (liberal Democrats and conservative Republicans) who are within 10 points of the party position have a .915 probability of running again, but those who are over 15 points from the party have a .722 probability of seeking office. Party moderates within 10 points of the state party position have a .883 probability of running, compared to a .609 probability for moderates over 15 points away. Essentially, most senators run again, but those who do not are likely to be farther from the state party position.

A number of factors besides the senator's voting record can affect both the decision to seek reelection and the success in getting reelected. Schmidt et al. (1996) used a multivariate regression (logit) procedure to take these other factors into account. In addition to distance from the party position, they controlled for the effects of the senator's age, the vote share when elected the first time, the strength of the member's party in the state and its success that year, and whether the state's other senator was from the same party. The senator's voting record continued to play a crucial role, even after accounting for these other effects. The probability of getting reelected dropped precipitously from .93 to .57 to .12 as the distance of the member from the state party position deviated 10, 19, and 28 ADA points, respectively.

We might speculate that some legislators could deviate without voter knowledge of the fact. Senators who are too liberal or conservative for their states will be penalized only if the voters discover the discrepancy. Because a greater percentage of educated voters are better informed about their senators' voting records (see Husted, Kenny, & Morton, 1995), there should be a greater penalty for deviating in those states where voters are more educated. Schmidt et al. (1996) found support for this reasoning. In states with more educated populations, the penalty is greater for accumulating a voting record that is either too liberal or too conservative. In other words, the probability of reelection decreases by a greater amount.

Conclusion

In sum, the evidence compiled in this chapter points to the significance of retrospective voting in guiding candidate behavior and to the divergent platform model as a superior way of accounting for the positioning of candidates on issues. This model can explain why elected officials from different parties draw support from different groups of voters in a district and have very different voting records in the legislature. Complaints that there is no difference between the two parties are thus unfounded.

The fact that candidates do not converge to the position preferred by the median voter does not mean that they can take any position without electoral repercussions. There may be some uncertainty about the distribution of voter preferences. Nevertheless, for any set of preferences there is a best platform or voting record for each party in a district. We have seen that senators who deviate too much from the state party position often choose not to seek reelection and, when they do run, are unlikely to be reelected. In the next chapter, we will show that only those House members whose ADA scores are close to the state party position are likely to win their party's nomination for the Senate. This in turn leads those who aspire to this higher office to modify their voting record over time to make it more acceptable to the state's electorate.

Notes

1. The interest groups publishing ratings on Congress include Americans for Democratic Action, the AFL-CIO's COPE, American Federation of Teachers, (U.S.) Chamber of Commerce, Christian Voice, Consumer Federation of America, League of Conservation Voters, National Alliance of Senior Citizens, and National Farmers Union.

2. Project Vote Smart's Web address: www.vote-smart.org

3. Downs (1957) suggested that voters can use a retrospective strategy to punish incumbents who support policies not preferred by the voters. Subsequently, Barro (1973), Ferejohn (1986), Austen-Smith and Banks (1989), Banks and Sundaram (1993), and Harrington (1993a, 1993b) developed theoretical models in which voters use retrospective strategies.

4. Although voters are unable to use a voting record in that office for nonincumbents, they often can refer to the candidate's record in some other office. If the candidate has never held political office, his or her party, political activity, and platform may offer clues about his or her future behavior.

5. Adding a second dimension does not result in many more votes being correctly classified. Accuracy rises by 3.0% to 83.6% in the Senate and by 1.7% to 84.4% in the House. The second dimension picks up different issues over time. When the second dimension was relatively influential (compared to other years), it captured disagreement over slavery, bimetallism, and civil rights. Additional dimensions add even less to our ability to explain congressional voting.

6. The distribution has the typical bell shape, which reflects the observation that very conservative or liberal preferences are typically less common than moderate preferences. The distribution's shape is not crucial in the analysis that follows.

7. See Barro (1973), Ferejohn (1986), Austen-Smith and Banks (1989), and Banks and Sundaram (1993).

8. For brief reviews of this literature, see Francis et al. (1994) and Schmidt et al. (1996).

9. Let us be more precise. If the distribution is symmetric and $M - R$ equals $D - M$, then each party is equally likely to win. If the distribution is not symmetric, the platforms will not be equidistant from the median if both parties are to be equally competitive.

10. Their sample excluded five states with 10 or fewer counties (Connecticut, Delaware, Hawaii, New Hampshire, and Rhode Island), Alaska (which did not have county voting data), and Louisiana (which had no general election).

11. If liberal and conservative candidates were equally likely to win any election, then two statewide elections per state will result in (a) two senators from the liberal coalition in one-quarter of the states, (b) two senators from the conservative coalition one-quarter of the time, and (c) a senator from each group in half the states. Thus, with equal odds of success, the divergent platform model predicts that the two senators will have different support groups in half the states. Different support groups are far more common, perhaps due to diminishing returns to a group's representation in the Senate.

12. Poole and Rosenthal (1997) reported that the correlation between the ADA (liberal) rating and their first dimension, which measures how conservative legislators are, is a very high −0.93 (p. 168).

13. The ADA counts absences the same as a vote against their position. Our corrected ADA score equals the votes supporting liberal causes divided by the number of votes cast. This avoids labeling Ted Kennedy as a conservative in 1980, when as a presidential candidate he missed 12 of the 18 votes used by the ADA. He supported liberal causes in the other 6 votes. The ADA gave him a 33, and we give him a 100. Peltzman (1984) and others have modified ADA scores in this fashion.

14. See Johannes and McAdams (1981), Glazer and Robbins (1985), Whitby and Bledsoe (1986), Abramowitz (1988), Westlye (1991), Goff and Grier (1993), and Wright (1993).

15. Between 1960 and 1990, Democrats controlled Arkansas, Louisiana, and West Virginia, and Republicans controlled Kansas. In addition, Alabama, Florida, Georgia, Montana, and Ohio reelected only Democrats.

16. The regression analysis explaining ADA scores was confined to senators who later were reelected.

17. That is, they estimated a separate regression for each state, which permits the distance between parties to vary from state to state. Whitby and Bledsoe (1986) also used party to predict legislators' voting, but with one regression for all states, they estimated a party difference that cannot vary from state to state.

6

Upward Mobility and Position Shifting

I n the preceding chapter, we argued that in each state there is an optimal ideological voting position for each party in statewide elections. Senators who are too liberal or too conservative do not get elected or reelected as often. By the same token, we may hypothesize that House members whose voting records are distant from the state party position are less likely to win a (statewide) Senate race. Republicans who represent very conservative House districts, for example, establish a very conservative voting record to ensure reelection in that district, but that same record may be too conservative for a successful Senate race. Similarly, moderate-to-liberal Republicans in up-scale suburban neighborhoods represent their districts' preferences well, but they may be too liberal to win the Republican Senate primary.

In this chapter, we examine the role that a U.S. representative's voting record plays in determining whether he or she runs for a Senate seat. We find that those who are far from the state party position *at the time of the Senate election* are much less likely to enter a Senate primary and to be named their party's candidate in the general election in November. But do House members who are close to the state position come from districts in which the district party position is close to the state party position? Or have Senate

97

hopefuls adjusted their voting behavior over time to become more acceptable in a statewide race? We find evidence that most Senate candidates have gradually shifted, over many years, toward the state party position.

U.S. House-to-Senate Mobility:
The Role of Voting Record

To examine these questions of House movement, we (Francis et al., 1994) evaluated all Senate elections in the time period 1960-1988 for the 41 states for which there was sufficient party competition to reelect senators from both parties. The sample consisted of 2,080 observations covering 345 elections, namely (a) all House members in a state each time there was an open Senate seat (i.e., no incumbent seeking reelection) and (b) if an incumbent sought reelection, only the House members in the state from the other party.[1]

The *state party position* in this particular study is simply the average corrected ADA score during the 1960-1992 period in the state and party of each senator.[2] In each state, there will be one score for Democrats and another score for Republicans. The distance of the House member's voting position from the appropriate state party position is defined as the absolute difference between the House member's ADA score in the previous congressional term and the state party position.

In 35 of the 41 states, a party's candidate in a general election was determined by a party primary. House members entered a Senate primary 106 times out of 1,840 opportunities, or 5.8% of the time; the 106 candidates are listed in Table 6.1. Of the 106 challenges, 81 of the candidates, or 76%, were selective enough to win the party primary.

In the remaining six states (Connecticut, Delaware, Indiana, Missouri, South Carolina, and Virginia), a convention is used to select the party's nominee for the general election. In 11 (or 4.6%) of the 240 observations from these states, House members became their party's candidate in the general election. These candidates also are listed in Table 6.1.

Forty-five of the 92 House members who ran in general elections won. Losers included four members who lost to a House member from the other party; obviously, in this situation, only one of the two House candidates could win. House members won 55% of the other 42 open races. Against incumbents, their record was poorer, as expected, but still surprisingly good: They were successful in 43% of such races.

Table 6.1   House Members From 36 States Who Ran for the U.S. Senate, 1960 to 1988

				Primary States	
State	Representative	Year	Party	Primary Winner	General Election Winner
Arizona	John Conlan	1976	Rep.	No	
	Sam Steiger	1976	Rep.	Yes	No
	John McCain	1986	Rep.	Yes	Yes
California	George Brown	1970	Dem.	No	
	John Tunney	1970	Dem.	Yes	Yes
	Alphonzo Bell	1976	Rep.	No	
	Robert Dornan	1982	Rep.	No	
	Barry Goldwater, Jr.	1982	Rep.	No	
	Paul McCloskey	1982	Rep.	No	
	Bobbi Fiedler	1986	Rep.	No	
	Ed Zschau	1986	Rep.	Yes	No
Colorado	William Armstrong	1978	Rep.	Yes	Yes
	Timothy Wirth	1986	Dem.	Yes	Yes
	Ken Kramer	1986	Rep.	Yes	No
Hawaii	Daniel Inouye	1962	Dem.	Yes	Yes
	Spark Matsunaga	1976	Dem.	Yes	Yes
	Patsy Mink	1976	Dem.	No	
Idaho	Gracie Pfost	1962	Dem.	Yes	No
	George Hansen	1968	Rep.	Yes	No
	James McClure	1972	Rep.	Yes	Yes
	Steven Symms	1980	Rep.	Yes	Yes
Illinois	Sidney Yates	1962	Dem.	Yes	No
	Roman Pucinski	1972	Dem.	Yes	No
	Paul Simon	1984	Dem.	Yes	Yes
Iowa	John Culver	1974	Dem.	Yes	Yes
	Charles Grassley	1980	Rep.	Yes	Yes
	Tom Harkin	1984	Dem.	Yes	Yes
Maine	William Hathaway	1972	Dem.	Yes	Yes
	William Cohen	1978	Rep.	Yes	Yes
	David Emery	1982	Rep.	Yes	No
Maryland	Daniel Brewster	1962	Dem.	Yes	Yes
	Charles Mathias	1968	Rep.	Yes	Yes
	Glenn Beall, Jr.[a]	1970	Rep.	Yes	Yes
	Paul Sarbanes	1976	Dem.	Yes	Yes
	Michael Barnes	1986	Dem.	No	
	Barbara Mikulski	1986	Dem.	Yes	Yes

(Continued)

Table 6.1   Continued

		Primary States			
State	*Representative*	*Year*	*Party*	*Primary Winner*	*General Election Winner*
Massachusetts	Laurence Curtis	1962	Rep.	No	
	Paul Tsongas	1978	Dem.	Yes	Yes
	James Shannon	1984	Dem.	No	
Michigan	Alvin Bentley[a]	1960	Rep.	Yes	No
	Robert Griffin[a]	1966	Rep.	Yes	Yes
	Marvin Esch	1976	Rep.	Yes	No
	James O'Hara	1976	Dem.	No	
	Donald Riegle	1976	Dem.	Yes	Yes
Minnesota	Clark MacGregor	1970	Rep.	Yes	No
	Donald Fraser	1978	Dem.	No	
Mississippi	Prentiss Walker[a]	1966	Rep.	Yes	No
	Thad Cochran	1978	Rep.	Yes	Yes
	Wayne Dowdy	1988	Dem.	Yes	No
	Trent Lott	1988	Rep.	Yes	Yes
Nebraska	John McCollister	1976	Rep.	Yes	No
	Harald Daub	1988	Rep.	No	
Nevada	Harry Reid	1986	Dem.	Yes	Yes
New Hampshire	Perkins Bass	1962	Rep.	Yes	No
	Chester Merrow	1962	Rep.	No	
	Norman D'Amours	1984	Dem.	Yes	No
New Jersey	Millicent Fenwick	1982	Rep.	Yes	No
New Mexico	Joseph Montoya	1964	Dem.	Yes	Yes
New York	Joseph Resnick	1968	Dem.	No	
	Richard McCarthy	1970	Dem.	No	
	Richard Ottinger	1970	Dem.	Yes	No
	Bella Abzug	1976	Dem.	No	
	Peter Peyser	1976	Rep.	No	
	Elizabeth Holtzman	1980	Dem.	Yes	No
North Carolina	N. Galifianakis	1972	Dem.	Yes	No
North Dakota	Tom Kleppe	1970	Rep.	Yes	No
	Mark Andrews	1980	Rep.	Yes	Yes
Oklahoma	Ed Edmondson	1972	Dem.	Yes	No
	James Jones	1986	Dem.	Yes	No

Table 6.1 Continued

			Primary States		
State	Representative	Year	Party	Primary Winner	General Election Winner
Oregon	Edwin Durno[a]	1962	Rep.	No	
	Robert Duncan	1966	Dem.	Yes	No
	James Weaver	1986	Dem.	No	
Pennsylvania	James Vanzandt	1962	Rep.	Yes	No
	Richard Schweiker	1968	Rep.	Yes	Yes
	William J. Green	1976	Dem.	Yes	No
	John Heinz	1976	Rep.	Yes	Yes
	Robert Edgar	1986	Dem.	Yes	No
South Dakota	George McGovern[a]	1960	Dem.	Yes	No
	James Abourezk[a]	1972	Dem.	Yes	Yes
	Larry Pressler	1978	Rep.	Yes	Yes
	James Abdnor	1980	Rep.	Yes	Yes
	Thomas Daschle	1986	Dem.	Yes	Yes
Tennessee	Ross Bass	1964	Dem.	Yes	Yes
	William Brock	1970	Rep.	Yes	Yes
	Ray Blanton	1972	Dem.	Yes	No
	Robin Beard	1982	Rep.	Yes	No
	Albert Gore, Jr.	1984	Dem.	Yes	Yes
Texas	George Bush	1970	Rep.	Yes	No
	Alan Steelman	1976	Rep.	Yes	No
	Robert Krueger	1978	Dem.	Yes	No
	James Collins	1982	Rep.	Yes	No
	Phil Gramm	1984	Rep.	Yes	Yes
	Ron Paul	1984	Rep.	No	
	Kent Hance	1984	Dem.	No	
	Beau Boulter	1988	Rep.	Yes	No
Utah	David King	1962	Dem.	Yes	No
	Lloyd Sherman[a]	1964	Rep.	No	
	Laurence Burton	1970	Rep.	Yes	No
	Wayne Owens[a]	1974	Dem.	Yes	No
Vermont	Richard Mallary	1974	Rep.	Yes	No
	James Jeffords	1988	Rep.	Yes	Yes
Washington	Don Bonker	1988	Dem.	No	
	Mike Lowry	1988	Dem.	Yes	No
Wyoming	Keith Thomson[a]	1960	Rep.	Yes	Yes
	Teno Roncalio[a]	1966	Dem.	Yes	No
	John Wold[a]	1970	Rep.	Yes	No

(Continued)

Table 6.1   Continued

| State | Representative | Convention States | | General Election Winner |
		Year	Party	
Connecticut	Hon. Seely-Brown[a]	1962	Rep.	No
	Lowell Weicker[a]	1970	Rep.	Yes
	Christopher Dodd	1980	Dem.	Yes
	Anthony Moffet	1982	Dem.	No
Delaware	William Roth	1970	Rep.	Yes
Indiana	Richard Roudebush	1970	Rep.	No
	Danforth Quayle	1980	Rep.	Yes
	Floyd Fithian	1982	Dem.	No
Missouri	Thomas Curtis	1968	Rep.	No
Virginia	William Scott	1972	Rep.	Yes
	Paul Trible	1982	Rep.	Yes

NOTE: Nine states that did not reelect at least one U.S. senator from each party were excluded. In addition, no House members from Alaska, Kentucky, Rhode Island, South Carolina, and Wisconsin entered their state's Senate primary or were selected by their state's nominating convention.

a. Due to insufficient data on ADA (Americans for Democratic Action) scores, these were not included in the analysis of changes in ADA scores as they approached their Senate bid.

From Francis et al., copyright 1994. Reprinted by permission of the University of Wisconsin Press.

Are the U.S. representatives whose voting records come closer to that of a typical senator from their own party indeed more likely to seek higher office?[3] In Table 6.2, members of the lower chamber are placed in two groups, those whose ADA scores are more extreme than that of the typical senator from their state party, and the centrists, whose ADA scores are more moderate. The proportion entering the primary at different distances from the state party position is given in the second and third columns of Table 6.2. It can be seen, for both the extreme and moderate groups, that House members closer to the state party position choose more often to run for the Senate. House members who are within 0 to 5 points of the state party position on the ADA scale, for example, are the most likely to challenge upward. The wing candidates, who are relatively liberal Democrats and conservative Republicans, as well as the centrist candidates, who are relatively conservative Democrats and liberal Republicans, are the least likely to enter a Senate primary.

Table 6.2   Mobility From the U.S. House to the Senate: Relationship Between Distance to Party Position and Probability of Primary Entry and Party Nomination

	Distance to Party Position	Primary Entry		General Election Candidate	
		Frequency	Sample	Frequency	Sample
Toward	25+	.033	215	.017	231
extreme	15-25	.033	214	.028	249
positions[a]	10-15	.052	191	.033	212
	5-10	.078	217	.071	254
	0-5	.112	205	.089	248
Toward	0-5	.103	165	.081	186
moderate	5-10	.063	128	.043	139
positions[b]	10-15	.050	101	.046	109
	15-25	.053	132	.032	155
	25+	.019	270	.010	295
Total			1,838		2,078

NOTE: Two observations in which distance to party position equaled zero were excluded.

a. Included are Democrats who are more liberal than predicted and Republicans who are more conservative than predicted.

b. Included are Democrats who are more conservative than predicted and Republicans who are more liberal than predicted.

From Francis et al. (1994). Reprinted by permission of the University of Wisconsin Press.

The data in Table 6.2 explain in part why the median voter model does not apply. The party primaries attract candidates who are close to one of the two state party positions, which in most states are substantial distances from each other. Because primaries are not attracting candidates from the middle of the state's political spectrum (who would appeal to the median voter), the divergent platform, or "two constituency," model is more appropriate. The effect of ideological distance is substantial. Those House members with ADA scores 10 to 15 points away from state party position are less than half as likely to enter a primary as are House members whose ADA scores are within 5 points of the party position. Because the parties in a typical state are about 50 points apart, divergent rather than similar positions will be taken by those members in opposing parties who seek to move up.

The last two columns in Table 6.2 report data on the actual nominees, consisting of those who won their party's primary and those who were selected by their party's convention. The choices of voters in primaries and conventions are consistent with expectations: That is, those whose ADA scores are closer to the state party position are more likely to be nominated.[4]

Of course, many other factors help determine whether a U.S. representative seeks higher office. We have in earlier chapters examined the impact on mobility from the House to the Senate of the member's wealth, power in the House, the number of House seats in the state (representing the number of potential competitors), and whether the seat was open. Although the details are not needed here, it may be pointed out that after statistically controlling for these and other factors, we continue to find that those who are far from the state party position are less likely to enter the primary and win the nomination.[5]

Head-to-Head Contests

Let us now return to the 106 who entered a Senate primary. This small sample reflects considerable self-selection. Those with better odds of winning are likely to take up the challenge. Eighty-three entered races in which they faced no opposition from another U.S. House member, and 71 (86%) of these House members won the primary.

Only 23 House members ran against another House member in a primary, including 10 primaries involving 2 members and an 11th primary with 3 members. The divergent platform theory predicts that the representative closest to the state party position will win; however, some races are no-calls. In 1982, Representatives Robert Dornan, Barry Goldwater, Jr., and Paul McCloskey, in a crowded California Republican primary, were defeated by Pete Wilson, then mayor of San Diego.[6] So there is no prediction here. The theory also makes no prediction about the outcome of the 1988 race in Washington in which Don Bonker and Mike Lowry were equally close to the Democratic state position.

The outcomes of the other nine head-to-head primary confrontations between U.S. representatives provide a suitable test of the importance of a candidate's record in determining success in upward mobility. Table 6.3 names the winners and losers and reports how close they were to the estimated winning position for their party. The winner was closer to the best position for the statewide race in seven of these nine elections and was, on average, 10 points closer, a difference that is statistically significant

Table 6.3 Outcomes of Contests Among Representatives in Senate Primaries

			Loser		Winner		
State	Year	Party	Name	Distance	Name	Distance	Difference
Arizona	1976	Rep.	Conlan	5	Steiger	1	−4
California	1970	Dem.	Brown	3	Tunney	9	6
California	1986	Rep.	Fiedler	22	Zschao	3	−19
Hawaii	1976	Dem.	Mink	13	Matsunaga	7	−6
Maryland	1986	Dem.	Barnes	5	Mikulski	1	−4
Michigan	1976	Dem.	O'Hara	21	Riegle	3	−18
New Hampshire	1962	Rep.	Merrow	41	Bass	9	−32
New York	1970	Dem.	McCarthy	12	Ottinger	14	2
Texas	1984	Rep.	Paul	19	Gramm	4	−15
						Mean	−10
							$(t = -2.51)$

NOTE: In 1982, Robert Dornan, Barry Goldwater, Jr., and Paul McCloskey ran in the California primary and were defeated by Pete Wilson, mayor of San Diego. In 1988, Mike Lowry defeated Don Bonker in the Washington Democratic primary. Both were equally close to the Democratic party position in Washington. Neither of these races is included in this table. *Distance* refers to distance from the state party position, the average ADA (Americans for Democratic Action) score for U.S. senators in that state and party.

From Francis et al. (1994). Reprinted by permission of the University of Wisconsin Press.

$(t = -2.51, p < .05$, one-tailed test). Primary voters are more likely to support those House members who are in fact closer to the state party position.

Position Shifting in Pursuit of Higher Office

We have seen that House members who are closer to the state party position at the time of the election are more likely to enter their party's primary and to be selected as their party's candidate in the general election. If the state party position is substantially more liberal or conservative than the constituency of a House member's smaller district, self-interest of the progressively ambitious members may call for a change in roll call voting patterns. It may lead those who aspire to higher office to shift away from the optimal record for winning in the smaller House district toward the optimal record needed to win the higher office.

Of course, this is done at some peril. Those who move too far from the district party position may be cast out of office before getting the chance to run for the Senate. The reelection mechanism in House district elections may be so effective that taking even small deviations from the district party position results in defeat. If so, candidates for higher office will not engage in position shifting until their last so-called "lame duck" term in the House—in other words, when they run for the Senate and no longer face defeat at the hands of their House district voters.

A contrary argument, often raised by supporters of term limits, is that legislators often deviate substantially from their districts, yet manage to get reelected. Some flexibility is obviously available to legislators, although Kingdon (1977, 1989) has made it clear that House members are very worried about district opinion. But deviating from the optimal record for a Senate race seems to be more costly than straying from the appropriate record for the House district, due to the more intense media attention given to U.S. Senate races and the fact that they often are more competitive than House races. Thus, those who anticipate seeking higher office may have the opportunity to deviate from what House constituents prefer and benefit from moving toward the state party position. They accordingly can be expected to make small shifts toward the voting position typically held by the U.S. senators in their state and party.

Earlier Studies

The early evidence on position shifting in the U.S. House was mixed. Hibbing (1986), in an analysis of elections spanning 24 years, ascertained that House members seeking a Senate seat did shift their voting between the first and second year of the term they ran for higher office. Members who were from districts that were more conservative (liberal) than the state as a whole typically had a more liberal (conservative) voting record in their last year in the House than the year before.[7] Carey (1994), using 20 years of House voting data, sought to explain whether members moved toward the average voting record of their state's House delegation over a 2-year term. He found greater shifting toward this "median" state position among the most liberal or most conservative members (by national standards) who were running for statewide office but found less shifting among the moderates.

Other studies of position shifting (e.g., Lott & Bronars, 1993; VanBeek, 1991; Zupan, 1990) generally find little evidence of a change in behavior in the last year or term prior to a bid for higher office. These studies, however, do not identify an optimal statewide position, a necessity if one is to determine whether a member of the House is shifting from the district's preferred position toward the statewide position in preparation for a run for statewide office.

We can expand the inquiry to settle these questions by asking not only whether House members who ran for the Senate tended to move toward a viable statewide position but also whether this movement occurred throughout their service in the House. The literature has focused on shifts in the voting record during the last term or entering into the last term. Such an approach incorrectly assumes that legislators risk deviating from district constituents' preferences only in the last term in the House, when they no longer seek reelection to their House seat, that state constituents are concerned only with their current behavior, or that House members do not plan very far ahead to run for higher office.

Evidence from at least two related studies, however, suggests that opinion leaders and voters take into account the candidate's record for the last several years when they evaluate performance in office.[8] Adams and Kenny (1989) found the success of governors in getting reelected depended on state income relative to predicted state income for the *entire term of office* and that success was unrelated to the growth of state income in the *year of the election*. Peltzman's (1990) findings also suggested that voters are not myopic and take account of elected officials' actions several years earlier. His statistical analysis found that incumbent parties are rewarded for low inflation and high income growth over a *3- to 4-year period prior to the election, not just the election year*. Such evidence underscores the importance that voters and party activists may attach to the credibility of candidate records. To display the consistency over time stressed by Downs (1957) and others, legislators aspiring to higher office may need to lay the groundwork well before the last term.

Here again, we use the average ADA scores for the years 1960-1992 for a party's U.S. senators in a state to calculate the state party position (Francis & Kenny, 1996). If there is statistical evidence that the party means have changed over time, then the period specific (1960-1976, 1977-1992) party mean is used.[9] We also again confine our analysis initially to the 41 states that in the years 1960-1992 reelected at least one U.S. senator from each party. The sample initially consisted of 106 House members who entered primaries, plus 11 who were selected by convention, who were described earlier in this chapter and are listed in Table 6.1. For this study, we had to eliminate those cases where there was not enough history from which to measure shifts (14 cases).[10] This left us with a sample of 103 House members from 35 states who sought a Senate seat.

Initial Positions

An initial voting record is needed to assess whether there has been any position shifting. The mean ADA score in a member's first term in office (or 1960 and 1961 if first elected to the House prior to 1960) is labeled *Initial ADA*. We can ask how many of the 103 House members were initially more liberal than the state Democratic party position and how many were between the state Democratic state party position and the "median voter" position. Likewise, we will want to know how many were more conservative than their state Republican party position and how many fell between the state Republican party position and the "median voter" position. The median voter is defined as the midpoint between the two party positions in each state. Thus, we can represent these ideological segments for a prototype state as follows:

where LD = liberal Democrat, sdp = state Democratic Party position, MD = moderate Democrat, mvp = median voter position, MR = moderate Republican, srp = state Republican Party position, and CR = conservative Republican. The actual positions sdp, mvp, and srp will vary from state to state and so will the proportion of members who fall into each segment.

Table 6.4 illustrates the distribution of the initial positions of 103 House members into the four segments. It should be understood that the length of each segment can vary by state. Clearly, House aspirants for the Senate straddle their own state party position and that (a) almost all Republican senatorial candidates have more conservative records than the estimated median voter position and (b) almost all Democrat candidates have more liberal records than the median voter position.

Very few candidates for higher office start off with a record that crosses the other party's position on the dimension. Two Democrats were no more than two points more conservative than the Republican position, and one Republican, Chester Morrow of New Hampshire, was nine points more liberal than the Democratic party position; Morrow, a clear party maverick, was not used in subsequent statistical analysis.[11]

Table 6.4   U.S. Representatives Who Later Ran for the Senate: Distribution of
Initial ADA[a] Scores

Party	More Conservative Than Republican Position	Republican Position to Median Position	Median Position to Democratic Position	More Liberal Than Democratic Position	Total
Democrats	2	4	16	28	50
Republicans	27	23	2	1	53
Total	29	27	18	29	103

a. ADA = Americans for Democratic Action.
From Francis and Kenny (1996). Reprinted by permission of the University of Wisconsin Press.

Movement From Initial Positions

We hypothesize that any position shifting will be toward the winning state party position. That is, we expect that the distance between the House member's ADA position and the winning Senate ADA position for the same party will *remain unchanged or decrease* as the member approaches a challenge for the Senate seat. Some House members will be very close initially to the optimal state position and will not need to improve their ideological position to run for statewide office. Others will need to move a considerable distance.

For each of the remaining 102 eventual Senate candidates, we use ADA scores from the first year the House member entered office (or 1960 if entry occurred earlier) until his or her Senate race, producing 795 observations. The regressions in Table 6.5 estimate how the distance from the state party position narrows as House members approach their bid for the Senate. The literature cited earlier has examined position shifting in only the last term of office, getting conflicting evidence on whether any shifting occurs. The first column in Table 6.5 shows that there is shifting in the last term, as some earlier studies suggested. Aspirants for the Senate are 2.3 ADA points closer to the state party position in the last term (i.e., the term in which they ran for the Senate) than in prior terms in the House.

If legislators assume, however, that voters are not myopic in assessing their record, they may well shift positions earlier than the term just prior to

Table 6.5 U.S. Representatives Who Later Ran for the Senate: Regressions Estimating Position Shifting as Bid Approaches (dependent variable = current distance from state party position)

Variable	(1)	(2)	(3)	(4)
Intercept	−1.177	−7.709	−11.067	−12.423
	(−0.14)	(−0.89)	(−1.26)	(−1.45)
Last term	−2.260	−3.813		
0-1 year left	(−2.65)	(−3.32)		
2-3 years left		−2.491		
		(−2.18)		
4-7 years left		−1.581		
		(−1.47)		
Time left			0.314	
			(3.00)	
Time left for extremists				0.065
				(0.58)
Time left for moderates				0.840
				(6.15)
Age	0.569	0.592	0.592	0.590
	(1.50)	(1.56)	(1.56)	(1.59)
Age^2	−0.0055	−0.0056	−0.0057	−0.0051
	(−1.34)	(−1.37)	(−1.38)	(−1.27)
Initial distance	0.600	0.602	0.603	0.604
	(16.96)	(17.04)	(17.06)	(17.45)
Adjusted R^2	.269	.277	.270	.300
Root mean square error	10.271	10.253	10.258	10.051
No. of observations	795	795	795	795

NOTE: t statistics are in parentheses.

From Francis and Kenny (1996). Reprinted by permission of the University of Wisconsin Press.

a bid for higher office. This is indeed what we find. The second regression contains three so-called "dummy" variables, indicating whether the House member is in the last term of office prior to a bid for the Senate (with 0 to 1 year left), is in the next-to-last term (with 2 to 3 years left), or has 4 to 7 years left.[12] The coefficient on Last Term implies that candidates are 3.8 points closer to the state party position in their last term than they were 8 or more years before their Senate bid. According to the coefficients on the other two dummy variables, 41% (1.581/3.813) of this movement has taken place by 4 to 7 years before the Senate race and 65% (2.491/3.813) by 2 to 3 years before the bid. Thus, position shifting starts well before the Senate race and appears to accelerate slightly as the bid draws near.

Time Left, used in the third regression in Table 6.5, provides a significantly better fit than the single dummy variable for the last term (first regression).[13] The evidence again suggests that House members move steadily toward their state party position as they approach a bid for the Senate. The coefficient on Time Left (.314) implies, for example, that Tim Wirth of Colorado was 3.45 points farther from his party position when he entered the House in 1975 than in 1986, the year he ran for the Senate (i.e., calculated as $3.45 = .314 \times (11 - 0)$, the regression coefficient $\times$ the number of years).

Further analysis (see Francis & Kenny, 1996) reveals that there is no shifting toward the optimal position until 13 years before a Senate bid. From then on, the distance from the state party position falls by .35 points per year, or 4.6 points over 13 years, as the election approaches. Because nine-tenths of our representatives were in the House no more than 13 years before they ran for the Senate, we can conclude that most of those who seek higher office begin moving toward the state party position as soon as they enter the House.[14]

It is possible that these results mask a movement toward the state median voter position instead of toward the state party position. To test for this possibility, we again separate aspirants for a Senate seat into party extremists (conservative Republicans and liberal Democrats) and party moderates (liberal Republicans and conservative Democrats), on the basis of their initial voting record relative to the state party position. Both the median voter and divergent platform spatial models predict that members will move from the extremes toward the center as they approach a Senate race. But do members also move from the center out to the winning party position, as asserted only by the divergent platform model? We can search for each type of movement by creating two variables that we will label Time Left for Moderates and Time Left for Extremists. These variables are entered for the last regression in Table 6.5.

The coefficient on Time Left for Extremists is not significant, indicating that the more liberal Democrats and the more conservative Republicans do not alter their voting records as the Senate election draws near. However, the coefficient on Time Left for Moderates is positive and significant. This means that *the moderates in each party do shift from the median voter position toward the divergent state party position.*[15] Thus, the results for Time Left for Moderates favor the divergent platform model over the median voter model.[16]

Let us now turn to the other determinants of distance from the state party position. The highly significant positive coefficients on Initial Distance imply that those who start off farther from the party position tend to be farther from this position throughout their career in the House. Because those who begin farther from the state party position must make a greater adjustment to have a "desirable" voting record, they should have a greater annual shift in their voting record. This means that there is interaction between the initial distance from the optimal position and the time left before challenging upward. Further regression tests, not detailed here, confirm the presence of this interaction.[17] Finally, the member's age is unrelated to distance from the party position when we control for the other initial distance and time remaining until a Senate bid.

Successful Candidates, Unsuccessful Candidates, and Noncandidates

Up to this point, we have not distinguished known aspirants from those who did not enter a Senate race nor have we distinguished winners from losers. In contrast to Senate candidates, those not aspiring to higher office have no need to appeal to a state constituency and indeed risk not getting reelected to their House seat if they do so. Accordingly, we hypothesize that *House members who entered Senate races are more likely to have shifted toward the state party position than House members who never ran for the Senate.*

As we saw in Chapter 5, Schmidt et al. (1996) found that U.S. senators far from the state party positions were less likely to seek and win reelection. Because being close to the party position is important to be successful in a Senate race, we hypothesize that *among House candidates to the Senate, winners are more likely than losers to have moved closer to the state party position.*

Three samples are employed to test these hypotheses: the 102 Senate candidates used in Table 6.5, the subsample of 40 who were elected to the Senate, and the 265 House members from Francis et al. (1994) who by 1992 had not run for the Senate.[18] For each of these samples, we estimate a bivariate regression coefficient *for each House member.* A member who receives a positive coefficient has moved toward the state party position. A member who receives a negative coefficient has moved away from the state party positions. Thus we may ask, in which subgroup do the highest percentage of members have positive coefficients? Our theory predicts it will be in the winning candidate group, with all candidates combined coming in second and noncandidates last.

Table 6.6   Estimating U.S. Representative-Specific Position Shifting as Bid Approaches: Comparison of Time Left Coefficients, by Party Noncandidates, Senate Candidates, and Winning Candidates

	Democrats			*Republicans*		
		Candidates			*Candidates*	
	Noncandidates	*All*	*Winning*	*Noncandidates*	*All*	*Winning*
No. of Cases	155	50	19	110	52	21
Coefficient						
% Positive	**41.9**	**64.0**	**73.7**	**57.3**	**63.5**	**71.4**
Prob. ≤ 0	.309	.001	.001	.002	.150	.156

SOURCE: Francis and Kenny (1996). Reprinted by permission of the University of Wisconsin Press.

In Table 6.6, Democrats and Republicans are separated. We see from the numbers in bold type that the results are consistent across parties. About 74% of the Democratic winners and 71% of the Republican winners had moved toward the state party position. Only 42% of the Democratic noncandidates and 57% of the Republican noncandidates had shifted toward the state party position. As expected, all candidates combined fall in between the other two groups.

The bottom row of the table reports the results of testing whether the group of coefficients is positive.[19] For Democrats, there is no evidence that noncandidates move toward the party position, but candidates clearly do. Among Republicans, even noncandidates move toward their respective state party position. During the time period analyzed, Republicans in the House were in the minority party, with seemingly little chance of gaining power or unseating a Democrat incumbent senator. Many may have seen other statewide or federal offices as a way to achieve their goals. Schansberg (1994) reported that Republicans were much more likely than Democrats to leave the House to pursue some higher office in the years 1969 through 1990, a period with mostly Republican presidents.

The results are not as consistent when each party is separated into party moderates and extremists in Table 6.7, where the subsamples are rather small. First, among liberal Democrats and conservative Republicans, candidates are more likely than noncandidates to approach the party position, and a greater

Table 6.7   Estimating U.S. Representative-Specific Position Shifting as Bid
Approaches: Comparison of Time Left Coefficients, by Party Moderate
and Extremist Noncandidates, Senate Candidates, and Winning Senate
Candidates

| | Moderate Democrats | | | Moderate Republicans | | |
| | | Candidates | | | Candidates | |
	Noncandidates	All	Winning	Noncandidates	All	Winning
No. of cases	76	22	10	28	25	11
Coefficient						
% Positive	**50.0**	**81.8**	**70.0**	**60.7**	**56.0**	**63.6**
Prob. ≤ 0	.181	.002	.003	.047	.523	.391
	Liberal Democrats			Conservative Republicans		
		Candidates			Candidates	
	Noncandidates	All	Winning	Noncandidates	All	Winning
No. of cases	79	28	9	82	27	10
Coefficient						
% Positive	**34.2**	**50.0**	**77.8**	**56.1**	**70.4**	**80.0**
Prob. ≤ 0	.572	.001	.001	.007	.069	.109

From Francis and Kenny (1996). Reprinted by permission of the University of Wisconsin Press.

percentage of winning candidates than candidates as a group shift toward the
optimal state position. Among moderate Democrats, candidates clearly distinguish themselves from noncandidates as expected, but winners and losers
are less distinct. Among moderate Republicans, the data are inconsistent.[20]

Conclusion

In this examination of the role of the legislator's voting record in upward
mobility, we have shown that U.S. House members who seek Senate seats do
in fact move toward the typical statewide ideological position taken by

senators from their own party and state. Three additional major results have added to our understanding of this phenomenon:

1. Movement toward a state party "winning" position begins at least a dozen years before the Senate bid, not 1 year or one term prior. Thus, U.S. representatives are not thrown out of office for small deviations from district voter preferences, and Senate hopefuls may spend their entire career edging toward the state party position.
2. Those aspiring to higher office are more likely to shift toward the state party position than are noncandidates.
3. Movement toward the state party position increases the odds of winning.

Does the position shifting that we observe matter? We find that winning Democratic and Republican candidates moved 6.6 and 3.0 points closer over four terms, narrowing the initial gap from the state party position by 57% and 34%, respectively (see Francis & Kenny, 1996).[21] It is clear from Table 5.2 (Chapter 5) that this shifting can noticeably improve the odds of winning a Senate race. In this chapter, it has been shown that those who were close to the state party position were much more likely to enter a Senate primary and to be named the party's standard bearer in the general election. Thus, we can conclude that Senate members are typically drawn from House districts that are ideal or nearly ideal for a statewide race. Position shifting helps those from nearly ideal districts become more viable candidates. But House members from districts with party positions 15 to 30 points from the state party position are unlikely, even with shifting, to become successful Senate candidates and thus are much less likely to seek higher office.

The evidence in this chapter, as in Chapter 5, is consistent with the divergent platform model and not with the median voter model. It is proximity to the party position, not the median voter position, that is rewarded in elections. Conservative Democrats and liberal Republicans, who are closer to the median voter, are less likely than members at the state party positions to enter a Senate primary and to be the party's nominee. Similarly, party moderates aspiring to the Senate tend to move to the party position, away from the median voter's preferred record. The results add to the evidence that in most states members do not behave as if there were one winning position common to both parties (i.e., the median voter position) but rather as if there were two divergent winning positions, one for Democrats and one for Republicans.

Notes

1. The latter restriction made data collection more manageable by ignoring the potential for incumbent U.S. senators to be challenged by U.S. representatives from their own party, which is very rare.

2. The average ADA score over 33 years is a crude measure of the state party position. Our results were unchanged when we used a predicted ADA score similar to that described in Chapter 5.

3. Grofman, Griffin, and Berry (1995) showed in a related study that House members who become senators have voting records that are similar to the average voting record for House members from their state and party.

4. Consistent with conventional wisdom about greater ideological variation among House members, a comparison of Tables 5.2 and 6.2 shows that there is much more variation in the ADA scores for a state party's House delegation than for the state party's Senate delegation. Forty-five percent of the House sample and only 15% of the Senate sample had ADA scores that were over 15 points from the state party position.

5. When the distance falls from its average value (17.7) to 0, the probabilities of entering the primary and being the party's nominee rise by 78% and 151%, respectively. Note that distance plays a stronger role in being selected as the party's standard bearer than in merely entering the primary.

6. Wilson was elected senator and later governor of California.

7. The political orientations of the state and district are measured by the share of the vote going to the Republican presidential candidates. The House member's legislative record is captured by the Conservative Coalition score.

8. On the other hand, Hibbs and other scholars have estimated that voters apply a very high discount rate on past economic performance in determining presidential approval (see Keech, 1995, p. 137). The weight voters apply appears to be 0.8 of the prior quarter's weight. This means that economic performance four quarters ago is worth $0.8^4 = 0.41 = 1/(1 + 1.43)$. That is, voters seem to be using a 143% annual discount rate.

9. Estimating a successful aspirant's movement toward a state party position could be contaminated if the measured party position included the candidate's later record as a U.S. senator. To avoid this problem, the state party average ADA scores have been modified for each successful candidate to exclude that candidate's Senate ADA scores.

10. This includes 3 who ran for the Senate in 1960, the first year of our ADA data, and 10 who sought higher office after their first term in the House. We also were unable to utilize Robert Griffin because he was the only Republican senator elected from Michigan.

11. Removing him has little impact on our results.

12. A search over the time span of the third dummy (i.e., 4 to 6 years, 4 to 8 years) produced the best fit at 4 to 7 years. This suggests that candidates start their journey toward the state party position well before their bid for the Senate.

13. A formal test of the difference in fit between two competing models is provided by the *J* test for non-nested models, which was proposed by Davidson and MacKinnon (1981). Our finding that predicted values from the Time Left regression are significant in the Last Term regression ($t = 1.76$) allows us to reject the hypothesis that shifting is better measured by Last Term. Similarly, the insignificance of predicted values from the Last Term regression in the Time Left regression ($t = 1.07$) does not reject the hypothesis that shifting is better captured by Time Left.

14. With two "spline" variables, the relationship between Time Left and the legislator's current distance from the party position is continuous and linear, and the slope is allowed to change once

at a cutoff year. We searched over cutoff years for the best fit and found that to occur at 13 years. The coefficient for the segment where Time Left > 13 is not significantly different from 0, and the coefficient for the segment where Time Left > 13, which equals 0.35, is significantly positive (see Francis & Kenny, 1996, p. 776).

15. If the moderate House members were shifting toward the median voter position and thereby away from the party position, the distance to the party position would be rising as time left diminished, implying a negative, not positive, coefficient.

16. The group we label party moderates includes 6 Democrats who were more conservative than the state median position and 2 Republicans who were more liberal than the median position. Because these 8 cross-median candidates were drawn toward the median position under both median voter and divergent platform models, we deleted them in an unreported regression to provide a more precise test of the median voter model against the divergent platform model. Doing so does not change the results.

17. To test for this, the regression included Time Left, Initial Distance, and the interaction of the two variables (Time Left × Initial Distance). The significantly positive coefficient on the interaction term ($t = 2.91$) is consistent with larger annual shifts toward the state party position when the Initial Distance is greater.

18. This "noncandidate" sample is drawn from the same 41 "two party" states for the years 1960 through 1988 and similarly requires at least three observations for each member. Republicans who initially had a more liberal record than even the state Democratic party and Democrats with a more conservative record than even the Republican party have been eliminated from the this sample. Because this sample uses data created for another study, there are some important differences between this and the two candidate samples. In the noncandidate data, ADA scores for each of a term's two sessions were averaged, reducing the noise in the data. The data also are not continuous over time because they were gathered only if there was a Senate election that term and the seat was open or not held by that party.

19. Table 6.6 reports the probability that the set of coefficients is not positive. We followed the meta-analysis literature and used the inverse chi-square test, known also as the Fisher test or the Pearson $P\lambda$ test, to assess overall significance. Let pi be the probability that the coefficient is, say, less than or equal to zero (the null hypothesis). Assuming that each coefficient represents an independent test of the null hypothesis, then it can be shown that $\Sigma -2 \bullet \log_e p^i$, $i = 1, 2, \ldots k$, has a χ^2 distribution with $2k$ degrees of freedom. This statistic is used to test the null hypothesis that the parameter is less than or equal to zero, based on evidence from the set of k regressions (see Hedges & Olkin, 1985).

20. We have not controlled for initial distance from the state party position or for the age of members in Tables 6.6 and 6.7 as we did in Table 6.5, which may account for some of the inconsistency here.

21. The median coefficients on Time Left were applied to a 7-year change. The average initial starting positions for Democrats and Republicans are 11.5 and 8.8 points, respectively, from the state party positions.

A Theory of Upward Movement

In this work, we develop a theory of political ambition that is more "goal specific" than in previous studies. To be sure, our political actors are "strategic politicians," who act rationally in manners similar to those described in the earlier works of Black (1972), Rohde (1979), or Jacobson and Kernell (1981) and to some extent anticipated by the previous works of Schlesinger (1966) and Downs (1957). Our strategic politicians seek to gain wider acceptance of their views and preferences by seeking office and then higher offices. But *higher* is an ambiguous term. We assert that acts of political ambition in the U.S. electoral system may be seen as attempts by political actors to increase their *territorial jurisdiction,* to increase the *size of their electoral constituency,* or both.

Goals and Moves

A wide array of offices, from local, nonpartisan town councils and school boards to highly partisan state and national offices, can be ordered in terms of their territorial jurisdiction and size of their electoral constituency:

1. Moves from local to state office or from state to national office increase territorial jurisdiction.
2. Moves from house to senate or from legislator to chief executive increase the size of the constituency.
3. Moves from mayor to governor or governor to president, or usually moves from local council to state legislature or from state legislature to Congress, increase both territorial jurisdiction and size of constituency.

These desirable changes in territorial jurisdiction and electoral constituency are reinforced by salary differences, for salaries tend to increase as jurisdiction and constituency rise. The political ladder that we observe reflects commonly held beliefs about the value of these offices in fulfilling these various goals.

Diversity and Professionalization: The State-Local Connection

Entry into politics varies considerably across the 50 states. In the more populous states, political careers tend to begin at the local level, where the costs of campaigning are less. Most who enter the state legislature in these urbanized states have held prior elective office or party positions. Their state legislatures tend to be more professionalized than in other states: That is, they pay higher salaries, offer more perks, have longer sessions, and generally demand a greater share of the member's time. In the sparsely populated states, where the so-called "amateur" or "citizen" legislatures are more frequent, most of the state legislators enter as relative novices. These are the "easy entry" state legislatures, whose elections are in districts with small populations and low campaign costs.

The literature on professionalization has tended to focus on the apparent characteristics of the state legislature itself. It is clear from our study that there is more to the story. The states with large urban areas and high population density are likely to have more layers of local government. The many local offices act as stepping-stones to the state legislature. Furthermore, states with large populations relative to the number of state legislative districts tend to offer legislators greater compensation and more perks. At the same time, the campaign costs required to win a state legislative seat in these same states are quite high. As a consequence, the more "professionalized" legislatures are more likely to attract local officials. They have had experience in local council-type legislatures and have some constituency funding base from which to launch a campaign. As Black (1972) pointed out in his study of local officials in the San Francisco area, public officials can transfer part of their investment in constituency support to the pursuit of higher office (p. 159). Local officials who move up to the state legislature may be more prone to treat politics as a career and thus to support a more professional legislature with salaries high enough to make "full-time" service possible.

Traditional Decisions to Climb the Political Ladder

Before term limits were imposed on many state legislatures, legislators appeared to be very selective in seeking higher office. Because it is difficult to unseat an incumbent, elected officials usually wait for open elections. Most elections have an incumbent running. For the years we cover, on average only 25% of state senate races, only 15% of U.S. House races, and only 27% of U.S. Senate races were open. Yet we find that house candidates for state senate seats in general elections were running for open seats 78% of the time. Almost 60% of state legislator primary races for a seat in the U.S. House were for open seats, and so were 59% of U.S. House member primary attempts for the U.S. Senate.

Open elections still can be risky if the candidate faces another quality candidate, such as someone with similar credentials. This leads many potential candidates for higher office to wait for the "right" open race, in which they will not face a serious challenge from another quality candidate. State house members run for the senate only 30% of the time that a senate seat is open. Because there are typically three house members who are potential candidates for any senate seat, only one of these generally ends up entering a senate race.

In other races, it may be more difficult to avoid running against another quality opponent. Because there are nine U.S. House districts in the average state, there are a large number of potential competitors for a Senate seat. Despite this, only 22% of House members entering a Senate primary faced another member of the House. There are 17 state legislative seats for every seat in the U.S. House. Not surprisingly, there are more head-to-head confrontations between state legislators running for Congress—between 30% and 46% of the races, depending on the time periods.

State senators in many states are able to run for higher office halfway through their 4-year senate term without risking their senate seat. Senators at midterm thus faced less risk of negative consequences in seeking higher office than senators at the end of their term, who would have to give up a senate seat to run for higher office, and they were in fact more than twice as likely to seek higher office. Perhaps due to less risk and their greater electoral base and experience, senators are two and a half times as likely as representatives to run for Congress. House members are expected to be more selective in choosing when to run because they seldom can run at midterm. And indeed, representatives are as successful as senators in winning, despite the disadvantages they face.

Changing Career Ladder Incentives Through Term Limits

The legislative term limits implemented between 1990 and 1995 are sometimes seen as affecting primarily state legislatures because the Supreme Court has prevented their application to Congress. Our thesis suggests that such a view is misleading. Term limits have catalyzed career movement in 18 states, from local to state and from state to national. In such states, careers can no longer be built by long and patient service in the legislative chamber. Typically, it is *up or out* in 6 to 8 years. Thus, opportunities will open more quickly for *local* officials who wish to increase their territorial jurisdiction. And members of the state legislature will be forced to challenge upward if they wish to progress in politics. As the evidence has shown, they will leave early frequently, perhaps to run for an open seat or to pursue another option. Strategically, many legislators will choose not to wait for the term limit deadline, when they may be forced to confront an incumbent in their bid for higher office. Timing may not be everything, but it certainly ranks near the top in political career decisions. Finally, the evidence indicates that the forced exodus from state legislatures is making congressional races more competitive than they have been.

Role of the Voting Record in Climbing
the Political Ladder

How do voters decide which candidate to support? Correspondingly, what determines which candidate wins an election? The candidate's experience, constituency service, and personality factors undoubtedly play a role, but so can the candidate's voting record. Will the voting record withstand scrutiny by constituents? Because most disagreement in politics may be captured by the conservative-liberal dimension, the legislator-contituency electoral relationship may boil down to whether the member has been too liberal or too conservative for the voters in the district. Various models of political competition predict that candidates who deviate too much from the preferences of some "decisive" voter are less likely to win the election.

The evidence to date on this issue comes from studies of Congress, for which there are numerous measures of how legislators have voted. We have shown that Senate members who are much more conservative or liberal than would be appropriate for a senator from their state and party are less likely (a) to win reelection and (b), recognizing this, to seek reelection. The elected official's record affects not only whether he or she stays in office but also whether advancement to higher office is feasible. House members whose votes locate them far from the optimal state party position are much less likely to run for the Senate and to be named their party's standard bearer in the Senate general election than are House members with the appropriate voting record. As a result, representatives from the most conservative or liberal districts in the state have difficulty advancing to a Senate seat.

Those who aspire to higher office recognize the importance of voting correctly. If they enter Congress with an ideological position dissimilar to the "winning" party position for the state as a whole, they will begin to alter their roll call voting positions in the direction of the state winning party position. Centrist Democratic House members whose statewide winning party position is liberal become more liberal, and centrist Republican House members become more conservative in states where the winning Republican position is more conservative. Likewise, Democrats and Republicans move to the center if the state winning position calls for it. Our political careerists are successful in making ideological adjustments to increase the size of their constituency. The extent of position shifting is limited, however, by the need to be reelected to the House district until a favorable opportunity for a Senate race arises.

Although our evidence is for Congress, we surmise that the candidate's voting record is important in any political race. It helps to determine who gets elected and reelected. Recognizing this, politicians continuously adjust their ideological position to enhance their political career.

Divergent Platforms

We have shown that for our purposes the *divergent platform* model works better than the *median voter* model. We are able to demonstrate that we get better estimates of who runs for higher office and who is more successful if we assume that each party in each state has a winning position, rather than assuming that there must be a single winning position common to both parties in the state. Our model does not preclude the possibility that the two parties could have the same winning position, but we find that in almost every state the Republican winning position is substantially more conservative than the Democratic winning position. This finding is consistent with the findings of Erikson, Wright, and McIver, who in 1989 reported consistent state-level divergences between Democrats and Republicans in their public opinion survey data.

Our evidence thus suggests that the spatial representation of ideological positioning is better described by assuming two divergent positions than by assuming a single median voter position. This divergence could be the product of a political system that requires candidates to first appeal to the party faithful to win a primary or convention nomination. Such a finding does not mean that the positions are divergent in some universal sense of far right to far left politics. From a global view, winning positions within each U.S. state look more like *competitive centrism* than extreme divergence. Within the context of what Americans see as viable, however, Democrats and Republicans clearly compete by taking distinctly different positions.

The party positions must be understood within the context of state politics. For both parties to be viable in state elections, each must take a position that appeals to enough voters in the state. Local political competition thus forces Republicans in liberal areas and Democrats in conservative areas to adopt moderate platforms that are less extreme than those taken in other parts of the country. This creates some ideological overlap between the parties.

Southern Democrats, for example, may be more conservative than New England Republicans. The state politics orientation of candidates and officials and the regional differences among Democrats or among Republicans are consistent with the findings from the earlier elite/mass opinion study of states by Erikson et al. (1989, 1993).

We might ask, how can two senators from the same state, such as Senators Graham and Mack in Florida, have divergent roll call voting records or Americans for Democratic Action (ADA) scores and yet win easily when they run for office? Part of the answer must lie in the different constituencies to which they appeal. Those who turn out to vote for Graham are not the same as those who turn out to vote for Mack. Still, realism must tell us also that there are some who vote for both, or even against both. Jung et al. (1994) argued that states often are represented by senators from both parties because of diminishing returns from representation. Florida Republicans, for example, have a smaller gain from having the second Republican senator than from having the first Republican senator representing their interests. As a result, Florida Republicans outspend Democrats in one Senate election and are outspent by Republicans in the other Senate election. Campaign spending, of course, helps to alter voters' opinions.

From another perspective, voters can be seen to take account of the candidate's integrity, experience, knowledge, appearance, stability, fairness, approachability, articulateness, and reputation for action or problem solving, as well as his or her voting record. The winning issue/attribute package of a Democratic candidate thus can be equally attractive to the same individual as the alternative winning package of a Republican candidate, yet not be the same.

The Rational Actor and Strategic Upward Movement

In seeking to gain greater acceptance of their views and preferences, political actors take into account a variety of factors, including the value of each office, the probability of winning each, the relative cost of running campaigns, and the ideological positioning necessary to win primaries and general elections. The perceived value of an office is determined primarily by its territorial jurisdiction and the size of its constituency base. Perceptions of the probability of winning an office are often affected by structural and situational conditions beyond the control of the aspirant, such as whether the seat is open, term limits, or the number of potential quality candidates within the jurisdiction. Upwardly mobile politicians, however, can directly affect the probability of winning. To do so, they can and will make adjustments in the policies they espouse. Supporting popular issues yields more votes in the next election directly and perhaps indirectly through positive effects on fund-raising, media coverage, and other opinion leader support. Politicians like to get their way on current policies, no doubt, but they may delay present gratification in return for future gains to be had in a more significant arena.

References

Abramowitz, A. (1988). Explaining senate election outcomes. *American Political Science Review, 82,* 385-403.

Abramson, P. R., Aldrich, J. H., & Rohde, D. W. (1987). Progressive ambition among United States senators: 1972-1988. *Journal of Politics, 49,* 3-35.

Adams, J. D., & Kenny, L. W. (1986). Optimal tenure of elected public officials. *Journal of Law and Economics, 29,* 303-328.

Adams, J. D., & Kenny, L. W. (1989). The retention of state governors. *Public Choice, 62,* 1-13.

Austen-Smith, D., & Banks, J. (1989). Electoral accountability and incumbency. In P. C. Ordeshook (Ed.), *Models of strategic choice in politics.* Ann Arbor: University of Michigan Press.

Banks, J., & Kiewiet, D. R. (1989). Explaining patterns of candidate competition in congressional elections. *American Journal of Political Science, 33,* 997-1015.

Banks, J., & Sundaram, R. K. (1993). Adverse selection and moral hazard in a repeated elections model. In W. A. Barnett, M. J. Hinich, & N. Schofield (Eds.), *Political economy: Institutions, competition, and representation.* Cambridge, UK: Cambridge University Press.

Barro, R. J. (1973). The control of politicians: An economic model. *Public Choice, 14,* 19-42.

Berkman, M. B. (1994). State legislators in Congress: Strategic politicians, professional legislatures, and the party nexus. *American Journal of Political Science, 38,* 1025-1055.

Black, G. S. (1972). A theory of political ambition: Career choices and the role of structural incentives. *American Political Science Review, 66,* 144-159.

Bond, J. R., Covington, G., & Fleisher, R. (1985). Explaining challenger quality in congressional elections. *Journal of Politics, 47,* 510-529.

Brace, P. (1984). Progressive ambition in the House: A probabilistic approach. *Journal of Politics, 46,* 556-571.

127

Brace, P. (1985). A probabilistic approach to retirement from the U.S. Congress. *Legislative Studies Quarterly, 10,* 107-124.

Campbell, J. E. (1993). *The presidential pulse of congressional elections.* Lexington: University Press of Kentucky.

Candidates for governor, senate, house. (1992, October 24). *Congressional Quarterly Weekly Report, 50,* 3415-3430.

Candidates for governor, senate, house. (1994, October 22). *Congressional Quarterly Weekly Report, 52,* 3062-3076.

Candidates for governor, senate, house. (1996, October 26). *Congressional Quarterly Weekly Report, 54,* 3089-3104.

Canon, D. T. (1990). *Actors, athletes, and astronauts.* Chicago: University of Chicago Press.

Carey, J. (1994). Political shirking and the last term problem: Evidence for a party-administered pension system. *Public Choice, 81,* 1-22.

Carey, J. M., Niemi, R. G., & Powell, L. W. (1998). The effects of term limits on state legislatures. *Legislative Studies Quarterly, 23,* 271-300.

Carey, J. M., Niemi, R. G., & Powell, L. W. (in press). *Term limits in state legislatures.* Ann Arbor: University of Michigan Press.

Cassie, W. E., & Breaux, D. A. (1998). Expenditures and election results. In J. A. Thompson & G. F. Moncrief (Eds.), *Campaign finance in state legislative elections.* Washington, DC: Congressional Quarterly.

Copeland, G. W. (1989). Choosing to run: Why House members seek election to the Senate. *Legislative Studies Quarterly, 14,* 549-566.

Daniel, K., & Lott, J. R., Jr. (1997). Term limits and electoral competitiveness: Evidence from California's state legislative races. *Public Choice, 90,* 165-184.

Davidson, R., & MacKinnon, J. G. (1981). Several tests of model specification in the presence of alternative hypotheses. *Econometrica, 49,* 781-793.

Downs, A. (1957). *An economic theory of democracy.* New York: Harper & Row.

Erikson, R. S., Wright, G. C., & McIver, J. P. (1989). Political parties, public opinion, and state policy in the United States. *American Political Science Review, 83,* 729-750.

Erikson, R. S., Wright, G. C., & McIver, J. P. (1993). *Statehouse democracy: Public opinion and policy in the American states.* Cambridge, UK: Cambridge University Press.

Fedderson, T. J. (1992). A voting model implying Duverger's law and positive turnout. *American Journal of Political Science, 36,* 938-962.

Fenno, R. F. (1978). *Home style.* Boston: Little, Brown.

Ferejohn, J. (1986). Incumbent performance and electoral control. *Public Choice, 50,* 5-25.

Fiorina, M. (1974). *Representatives, roll calls, and constituencies.* Lexington, MA: Lexington Books.

Fowler, L. L. (1979). The electoral lottery: Decisions to run for Congress. *Public Choice, 34,* 399-418.

Francis, W. L. (1993). House to Senate career movement in the U.S. states: The significance of selectivity. *Legislative Studies Quarterly, 18,* 309-320.

Francis, W. L., & Kenny, L. W. (1996). Position shifting in pursuit of higher office. *American Journal of Political Science, 40,* 768-786.

Francis, W. L., & Kenny, L. W. (1997). Equilibrium projections of the consequences of term limits upon expected tenure, institutional turnover, and membership experience. *Journal of Politics, 59,* 240-252.

Francis, W. L., Kenny, L. W., & Anderson, B. (1998, March). *The churning of membership in state legislatures: Effects of term limits and anticipatory behavior.* Paper presented at the annual meeting of the Public Choice Society, New Orleans, LA.

Francis, W. L., Kenny, L. W., Morton, R. B., & Schmidt, A. B. (1994). Retrospective voting and political mobility. *American Journal of Political Science, 38,* 999-1024.

Freeman, P. K. (1995). A comparative analysis of speaker career patterns in U.S. state legislatures. *Legislative Studies Quarterly, 20,* 365-376.

Garand, J. C. (1991). Electoral marginality in state legislative elections, 1968-86. *Legislative Studies Quarterly, 16,* 7-28.

Glazer, A., & Robbins, M. (1985). How elections matter: A study of U.S. Senators. *Public Choice, 46,* 163-172.

Goff, B. L., & Grier, K. B. (1993). On the (mis)measurement of legislator ideology and shirking. *Public Choice, 76,* 5-20.

Green, J. C. (1996). A re-examination of the role of money in congressional elections: Open seat elections from 1982-1992. *Southeastern Political Review, 24,* 301-331.

Grier, K. B. (1989). Campaign spending and Senate elections. *Public Choice, 63,* 201-220.

Grofman, B. (Ed.). (1996). *Legislative term limits: Public choice perspectives.* Boston: Kluwer Academic.

Grofman, B., Griffin, R., & Berry, G. (1995). House members who become Senators: Learning from a "natural experiment" in representation. *Legislative Studies Quarterly, 20,* 513-529.

Grofman, B., Griffin, R., & Glazer, A. (1990). Identical geography, different party: A natural experiment on the magnitude of party differences in the U.S. Senate, 1960-84. In R. J. Johnston, F. M. Shelley, & P. J. Taylor (Eds.), *Developments in electoral geography.* London: Routledge.

Grofman, B., & Sutherland, N. (1996). Gubernatorial term limits and term lengths in historical perspective, 1790-1990: Geographic diffusion, non-separability, and the ratchet effect. In B. Grofman (Ed.), *Legislative term limits: Public choice perspectives.* Boston: Kluwer Academic.

Hain, P. L., Roeder, P. G., & Avalos, M. (1981). Risk and progressive candidacies: An extension of Rohde's model. *American Journal of Political Science, 25,* 188-192.

Harrington, J. (1993a). Economic policy, economic performance, and elections. *American Economic Review, 83,* 27-42.

Harrington, J. (1993b). The impact of reelection pressures on the fulfillment of campaign promises. *Games and Economic Behavior, 5,* 71-97.

Hedges, L. V., & Olkin, I. (1985). *Statistical methods for meta-analysis.* Orlando, FL: Academic Press.

Hibbing, J. R. (1986). Ambition in the House: Behavioral consequences of higher office goals among U.S. Representatives. *American Journal of Political Science, 30,* 651-665.

Hogan, R. E., & Hamm, K. E. (1998). Variations in district-level campaign spending in state legislatures. In J. A. Thompson & G. F. Moncrief (Eds.), *Campaign finance in state legislative elections..* Washington, DC: Congressional Quarterly Press.

Huntington, S. (1950). A revised theory of American party politics. *American Political Science Review, 44,* 669-677.

Husted, T. A., Kenny, L. W., & Morton, R. B. (1995). Constituent errors in assessing their Senators. *Public Choice, 83,* 251-271.

Jacobson, G. C., & Kernell, S. (1981). *Strategy and choice in congressional elections.* New Haven, CT: Yale University Press.

Jewell, M., & Breaux, D. (1988). The effect of incumbency in state legislative elections. *Legislative Studies Quarterly, 13,* 495-514.

Jewell, M., & Breaux, D. (1991). Southern primary and electoral competition and electoral success. *Legislative Studies Quarterly, 16,* 129-144.

Johannes, J. R., & McAdams, J. C. (1981). A congressional incumbency effect: Is it casework, policy compatibility, or something else? An examination of the 1978 election. *American Journal of Political Science, 25,* 512-542.

Jung, G., Kenny, L. W., & Lott, J. R., Jr. (1994). An explanation for why Senators from the same state vote differently so often. *Journal of Public Economics, 54,* 65-96.

Keech, W. R. (1995). *Economic politics: The costs of democracy.* Cambridge, UK: Cambridge University Press.

Kenny, L. W., & Rush, M. (1990). Self-interest and the Senate vote on direct elections. *Economics and Politics, 2,* 291-302.

King, J. D. (1997, November). *Changes in professionalism in American state legislatures.* Paper presented at the annual meeting of the Southern Political Science Association, Norfolk, VA.

Kingdon, J. W. (1977). Models of legislative voting. *Journal of Politics, 39,* 563-595.

Kingdon, J. W. (1989). *Congressmen's voting decisions.* Ann Arbor: University of Michigan Press.

Krasno, J. S., & Green, D. P. (1988). Preempting quality challengers in House elections. *Journal of Politics, 50,* 920-936.

Lott, J. R. (1996). *A simple explanation for why campaign expenditures are increasing: The government is getting bigger.* Working paper.

Lott, J. R., Jr., & Bronars, S. G. (1993). Time series evidence on shirking in the U.S. House of Representatives. *Public Choice, 76,* 125-149.

McClosky, H., Hoffman, P. J., & O'Hara, R. (1960). Issue conflict and consensus among party leaders and followers. *American Political Science Review, 54,* 406-427.

Miller, W. E., & Jennings, M. K. (1986). *Parties in transition: A longitudinal study of party elites and party supporters.* New York: Russell Sage Foundation.

Moncrief, G. F. (1998). Candidate spending in state legislative races. In J. A. Thompson & G. F. Moncrief (Eds.), *Campaign finance in state legislative elections.* Washington, DC: Congressional Quarterly Press.

Moncrief, G. F., Thompson, J. A., Haddon, M., & Hoyer, R. (1992). For whom the bell tolls: Term limits and state legislatures. *Legislative Studies Quarterly, 17,* 37-47.

Morton, R. B. (1987). A group majority voting model of public goods provision. *Social Choice and Welfare, 4,* 117-131.

Mullaney, M. M. (1994). *Biographical directory of the governors of the United States: 1988-1994.* Westport, CT: Greenwood.

Opheim, C. (1994). The effects of U.S. state legislative term limits revisited. *Legislative Studies Quarterly, 19,* 49-59.

Palfrey, T. R. (1984). Spatial equilibrium with entry. *Review of Economic Studies, 51,* 139-157.

Peltzman, S. (1984). Constituent interest and congressional voting. *Journal of Law and Economics, 27,* 181-210.

Peltzman, S. (1990). How efficient is the voting market? *Journal of Law and Economics, 33,* 27-64.

Petracca, M. P., & O'Brien, K. M. (1996). The experience in municipal term limits in Orange County. In B. Grofman (Ed.), *Legislative term limits: Public choice perspectives.* Boston: Kluwer Academic.

Poole, K. T., & Rosenthal, H. (1997). *Congress: A political-economic history of roll call voting.* Oxford, UK: Oxford University Press.

Polsby, N. W. (1968). Institutionalization of the U.S. House of Representatives. *American Political Science Review, 62,* 144-169.

Robeck, B. W. (1982). State legislator candidacies for the U.S. House. *Legislative Studies Quarterly, 7,* 507-514.

Rohde, D. W. (1979). Risk-bearing and progressive ambition: The case of the United States House of Representatives. *American Journal of Political Science, 23,* 1-26.

Rosenthal, A. (1996). State legislative development: Observations from three perspectives. *Legislative Studies Quarterly 21,* 169-198.

Schansberg, D. E. (1994). Moving out of the House: An analysis of congressional quits. *Economic Inquiry, 32,* 445-456.

Schlesinger, J. (1966). *Ambition and politics: Political careers in the U.S.* Chicago: Rand McNally.

Schmidt, A. B., Kenny, L. W., & Morton, R. B. (1996). Evidence on electoral accountability in the U.S. Senate: Are unfaithful agents really punished? *Economic Inquiry, 34,* 545-567.

Squire, P. (1988). Career opportunities and membership stability in legislatures. *Legislative Studies Quarterly, 13,* 65-82.

Squire, P. (1989). Challengers in U.S. Senate elections. *Legislative Studies Quarterly, 14,* 531-548.

Squire, P. (1992). Legislative professionalism and membership diversity in state legislatures. *Legislative Studies Quarterly, 17,* 69-79.

Stewart, C., III. (1989). A sequential model of U.S. Senate elections. *Legislative Studies Quarterly, 14,* 567-602.

VanBeek, J. R. (1991). Does the decision to retire increase the amount of political shirking? *Public Finance Quarterly, 19,* 444-456.

Westlye, M. C. (1991). *Senate elections and campaign intensity.* Baltimore: Johns Hopkins University Press.

Whitby, K. J., & Bledsoe, T. (1986). The impact of policy voting on the electoral fortunes of Senate incumbents. *Western Political Quarterly, 39,* 690-700.

Wright, M. B. (1993). Shirking and political support in the U.S. Senate, 1964-84. *Public Choice, 76,* 103-123.

Zupan, M. A. (1990). The last period problem in politics: Do congressional representatives not subject to a reelection constraint alter their voting behavior? *Public Choice, 65,* 167-180.

Index

About the Authors

Wayne L. Francis is Professor of Political Science at the University of Florida, where he has taught since 1986. He previously held positions at the University of Missouri, University of Washington, and Syracuse University. He received his B.A. from Wabash College and his M.A. and Ph.D. from Indiana University. In recent years, he has served as Co-Editor of *Legislative Studies Quarterly* and as Chair of the Legislative Studies section of the American Political Science Association. His research has focused on the study of legislators and legislatures and on the modeling and interpretation of data. He conducted the first scholarly nationwwide survey of state legislators in 1963, resulting in his book *Legislative Issues in the Fifty States* (1967). Since then, he has coauthored or authored several books, including *Political Research: Design, Measurement and Analysis* (1974) and *The Legislative Committee Game* (1989). He has published articles in *American Journal of Political Science, American Political Science Review, Journal of Politics, Legislative Studies Quarterly, Western Political Quarterly, Policy Studies Journal, Simulation and Games,* and *Quality and Quantity.*

Lawrence W. Kenny is Professor of Economics and Affiliate Faculty Member of Political Science at the University of Florida, where he has taught since 1975. He has been a Visiting Scholar with the National Bureau of Economic Research. He earned a B.A. from Wesleyan University and an M.A. and Ph.D.

from the University of Chicago. His research has addressed a number of topics of interest to both economists and political scientists: voter information and turnout, city-county consolidation, redistribution, government spending, term limits on governors and legislators, political careers, the role of elections in rewarding good officials and punishing those who are poor agents of the voters, spatial competition, the determination of the number of jurisdictions, private schooling, state involvement in the primary and secondary school system, and the mix of taxes chosen by governments. He has published articles on this research in leading political science journals (e.g., *American Journal of Political Science, Journal of Politics*), interdisciplinary journals (e.g., *Public Choice, Economics and Politics*), and in prominent economics journals (e.g., *Journal of Political Economy, Economic Inquiry, Journal of Law and Economics, Journal of Public Economics*). He serves on the editorial board of *Economic Inquiry.*